TILLA
22

SUBSCRIPTIONS

SCINTILLA 16 and all later issues can be purchased through
Amazon.com or Amazon.co.uk.
For convenience, we hope to make back issues
available through Amazon in future.
Issues 1-15 are available directly from The Vaughan Association.
Please email subscriptions@vaughanassociation.org to get further details.

*

WEBSITE

www.vaughanassociation.org

EMAIL

subscriptions@vaughanassociation.org

Submissions for Scintilla 23

Please submit critical articles on literature
in the metaphysical tradition to
prose@vaughanassociation.org.

Please submit new poetry for consideration to
poetry@vaughanassociation.org.

All submissions are peer reviewed

SCINTILLA

The Journal of the Vaughan Association

22

Thus all is hurl'd
In sacred *Hymnes*, and *Order*, The great *Chime*
And *Symphony* of nature.

Henry Vaughan, *The Morning-watch*

I Think it were more *plaine*, and to some *Capacities* more *pleasing*, if I should *expresse* my self in this popular, low *Dialect*.

Thomas Vaughan, *Lumen de Lumine*

A journal of literary criticism, prose and new poetry
in the metaphysical tradition

Published by
The Vaughan Association

Published in 2019
Scintilla is a publication of The Vaughan Association

Some of the essays in each issue of *Scintilla* originate in talks first given at The Vaughan Association's annual Colloquium held over the last full weekend in April near the Vaughans' birth-place at Newton Farm near Llansantffraed, Breconshire.

ISBN: 978-1-09-198474-5
ISSN 1368-5023

Published with the financial support of the Welsh Books Council

Typeset in Wales by the Dinefwr Press, Rawlings Road, Llandybïe, Carmarthenshire, SA18 3YD
Printed by Kindle Direct Publishing

Contents

Preface

In *Scintilla 22* we continue this journal's tradition of exploring and extending the literary legacy of the Vaughan brothers and their literal and figurative poetic peers. These identical twins, who were shaped by the beauty of the Breconshire of their youth, continually returned to their memories of the Usk river valley with its unique features: gently rolling hills and dense groves filled with flora and fauna, stones and rivers, history and myths. This landscape ignited their imaginations, as they sought to endure the social and political changes that swirled around them in seventeenth-century England. Their experiences with the horror of civil unrest, the erasure of familiar political and religious institutions, the struggle to retain identity and continuity, all marked these writers and their works. As Henry and Thomas reinvented themselves (Henry as 'Silurist' and Thomas as 'Eugenius Philalethes'), their creative works explored the relationships among identity, adversity, and the creative processes in their writing. *Scintilla* continues that tradition of probing these conjunctions and crossing boundaries between past and present; between place and vision; between our physical environment and our inner lives; between metaphysical experiences and the concrete language of science, poetry, and healing.

In this issue, we are pleased to share a series of wonderful articles. Jonathan Post examines Henry Vaughan's poems in the light of movement and walking and places his poetry in the context of this tradition, one that includes other writers, such as Henry David Thoreau and Robert Frost. Elizabeth Siberry documents and demonstrates how nineteenth century Welsh readers exhibited a deeper understanding and wider appreciation for Henry Vaughan's poetry than we have thought. Mai Matsumoto explores how Vaughan employs the operation of magnetic power as a representation of his wider range of religious beliefs, such as when he describes the resurrection of the body. Jonathan Naumann traces the influence of Christian Platonism broadly, and Boethius' *Consolation of Philosophy* in particular, on Vaughan's poetic sensibility.

It is an abiding interest of *Scintilla* to explore the people and texts that surround the Vaughan brothers and their milieu. To that end, Sean McDowell explores George Herbert's ongoing effort to redeem the sonnet from the service of secular love and explore other emotions and purposes beyond those predominating in the Petrarchan mode. Finally, Vicki Kay introduces our readers to Lady Brilliana Harley, whose life and letters capture the complexity and the calamities that define England's Civil War period.

As it has for the past decade, *Scintilla* continues to extend its reach exploring the variety of poets and thinkers who write in the metaphysical tradition. *Scintilla 22* offers important reflections, not only on poets such as Henry Vaughan and David Jones who have frequently been subjects of interest in our pages, but introduces a number of lesser known poetic voices.

Many of the poems chosen for this issue of *Scintilla* feature a sense of being poised on the edge of transformation, and whilst there is celebratory anticipation of renewal, there is also room for necessary doubt and self-deprecation regarding our capacity to change and the resilience needed for it. For the titular speaker of Rosie Jackson's poem 'An Anchorite Laments the Destruction of her Cell, 1537', in the shock of the newly-external world 'days are too bright, / stars too sharp, prayers too feeble to be heard over such / great distances'. The natural world offers no amplification for devotion and she urges her protector to 'return me / to the discipline of the squint, the blind comfort of darkness'. In one of Margaret Wilmot's two poems included here, it's the act of stepping out that brings the benefit, the 'worth': 'the scrubby waste was washed / with gold – and she too gilded'. The 'gold' in question is a goldenrod plant which has found a way to thrive amid 'an unkempt space'. Such forceful abundance is also to be found in Séan Street's poem: 'Morning cutting / down into rock / always finds voice', the voice of birdsong, carved.

But to sing is not always to know, as a number of poems remind us, including 'Showing, Not Telling' by Lesley Saunders, in which a 'white-faced owl / is asking to be lip-read as psyche, as cipher or semaphore, / a child's name in the ark of a mother's mouth'. The poem ends with the playful, elliptical assertion, 'I knew you were you all along'. To know is to un-know, as Paul Connolly cheerfully reminds us, when a woodland walk allows a man to 'plot / himself anew in knowing that's renewal / and motion,' but we end with the wry undermining of the act: 'if knowing's anything at all'.

Walking with Vaughan in *Silex Scintillans*

JONATHAN F. S. POST

"It is as though the earthly church had vanished, and man were left to walk alone with God."
– Louis L. Martz, *The Paradise Within: Studies in Vaughan, Traherne, and Milton*

The title of my paper indicates its general direction, but before setting out, and in keeping with its roving spirit, I want to begin with a few words about my only other pilgrimage to Vaughan country, now forty years ago. In almost every respect, it was a more primitive event. There was nothing so inviting then as a 'Vaughan Walk', nor as welcoming as the recent collection of essays and photos handsomely assembled by Elizabeth Siberry and Robert Wilcher in *Henry Vaughan and the Usk Valley*. The Llansanffraed church was locked; Vaughan's grave was in shadows, under a yew tree, I believe; and I was about as green an academic as you could be. Having received some money from Yale for research at the University of Cardiff library, I simply showed up at the door, not having written a letter in advance, only to discover what became immediately obvious: that the library was closed for the week for inventory. I knocked – pounded, rather – in desperation on the front door. Eventually, a perplexed face appeared on the other side of the glass. We mimed a conversation of sorts that was going nowhere until I held up to view a letter from my department chair, briefly explaining my reasons for being there.

That was the summer of 1977. As were many at the time, I had been greatly influenced by Christopher Hill's writings, especially *The World Turned Upside Down*. Among Hill's revolutionary heroes – and the Civil War marked a revolution in Hill's eyes – were the radical Welsh millenarians, William Erbery and Vavasour Powell, whose works were in the Cardiff Library. The librarian, whose name I shouldn't recall if I could, cautiously, courteously, opened the door. I was admitted. For the next two days, I had free access to the relevant stacks of rare books while he worked elsewhere on his inventory. I was so embarrassed and grateful that it never occurred to me to pocket a single one of the library's treasures. My major takeaway, rather, was discovering the writings of Thomas Richards, the father of modern history of South Wales.

In 1977, Vaughan was hardly the civil-war poet he has become today. He was read largely according to the canons of New Criticism and for his ties with the world of the occult, whether perceived as Hermetic or Mystical, and occasionally as a neo-Romantic. In many quarters, he was still valued as the author of arresting lines. In 1978, the American poet, James Merrill, concluded the 'Mirabel' section of what was to become his epic poem, *The Changing Light at Sandover*, with 'Vaughan's unbeatable | "They are all gone into a world of light,"' the opening line, that is, of the poem that goes by that title. Unbeatable but also beaten about a bit as Merrill slightly misquotes Vaughan's line. As Vaughan readers will recognize, the original reads more emphatically '*the* world of light,' not '*a* world of light.' Nonetheless, it *is* a great line. Robert Lowell thought so too, although he too made the same mistake while quoting the line in his elegy for his grandparents in his watershed book of confessional poems, *Life Studies*, published in 1959, and the likely source of Merrill's error. Still, it is good to have poets of this caliber in your corner. It is also entirely characteristic of Merrill's doubled-handed way with words if we hear in his use of 'unbeatable' his admiration for Vaughan's metrical habits. 'Unbeatable' in the sense that the line avoids the ta dum, ta dum regular *beat* of iambic feet, opting rather for something more prosodically varied and enchanting, in which the stress probably falls out as follows: 'they are **all gone in**to the **world** of **light**!'

But is the line unbeatable in the obvious sense that Merrill meant – that is, unrivalled, not to be bested? A matter of taste perhaps, but anticipating the direction of my essay, I admit to being equally taken by the visionary flair of the opening, also metrically inviting, line of the third stanza, 'I see them walking in an Air of glory', as if Vaughan were commenting on a painting by Fra Angelica or Giovanni Bellini, where such images routinely occur.[1] But not in nature, let alone on 'this hill', the hill apparently within Vaughan's view. Here the line gathers force by the trochaic stress on the medial present participle 'walking' (echoed in the closing trochee 'glory') and the double sense of agency expressed: the poet seeing, the people walking. Lyric poetry often gets its quickness through the emphatic use of present tense – its rush of sudden awakening – and does so on this occasion, in which Vaughan's first-person 'I' and his visionary 'eye' become ours too.

Since 1977, the idea of Vaughan as a civil-war poet has acquired much steam in scholarly circles, in keeping with the political turn of literary studies more generally, and it is perhaps culminating in the admirably learned, detailed

1 References to Vaughan's writing are to *The Works of Henry Vaughan*, ed. Donald R. Dickson, Alan Rudrum, and Robert Wilcher. 3 vols. Oxford: Clarendon Press, 2018), 2: 568.

writings of Robert Wilcher and the new Oxford edition of Vaughan's *Works*. What follows does not discount the significance of these historical events any more than it questions the depth of Vaughan's response to their painful effects. The layering of the political and the religious on to the personal, the loss of crown, church, and family, is one of the special attributes of *Silex Scintillans*. It deepens and propounds the experience of deprivation sounded in the poetry and the corresponding urgent wish by the poet to be delivered from the world of pain and care, in which, quoting Job in the epigraph to the completed *Silex* in 1655, Vaughan seeks to give 'Songs in the night.' But my approach is more phenomenological and impressionistic than it is explicitly historical. That is, it is about how Vaughan, as a lyric poet, imagined navigating through this period of his life, literally, by thinking about movement in general in his poetry, and specifically, in many instances, about the subject of walking itself. My hope is, along the way, to claim a significant place for Vaughan in the history of walking, one nearly on a par with that great ambler William Wordsworth, whom Vaughan anticipates in a number of ways, and, in the process, to shed some new light on Vaughan's poetry.[2] My mantra is borrowed from Wallace Stevens' *Notes Toward a Supreme Fiction* that 'to impose is not to discover'; 'perhaps | the truth depends on a walk around a lake.'[3] The advice seems especially pertinent to the genre of lyric in which images of landscape figure so prominently and the idea of arriving is often as important as the finish itself.

Centuries later, with the examples of long-lived poets such as Wordsworth and Yeats in mind, readers often think of Vaughan's poetic activity as brief, an intense blip of about six or so years, and wonder why it is he spent himself so quickly. But, surely, that is not how events appeared to him in his poetry, wherever it was composed, as he imagined travelling ecstatically forward in 'The Search' or drunkenly backward in 'The Retreate' or as he numbly counted the 1200 hours since his brother William's death in 'Silence, and stealth of dayes!'. 'My walke', Vaughan precipitously notes at the outset of *Silex Scintillans*, in 'Regeneration', is 'a monstrous, mountain'd thing | Rough-cast with Rocks, and snow'.[4] And corresponding to this roughness, we know from the plain, unvarnished plea in 'Anguish' how he felt about writing poetry during these

2 For Wordsworth's renowned place among poets in the history of walking see Rebecca Solnit, *Wanderlust, A History of Walking* (2001; Granta Books, 2014), ch. 7 ("The Legs of William Wordsworth").

3 Wallace Stevens: *The Collected Poems* (New York: Vintage Books, 1954), 403. The same quotation and critical rationale underlie my essay "'On each pleasant footstep stay': A Walk about 'Appleton House,'" The *Ben Jonson Journal* 11 (2004): 163-205. I have written elsewhere about walking in "Footloose in Paradise: Masaccio, Milton, and Renaissance Realism," *The Huntington Library Quarterly* 69 (2006), 403-23.

4 *The Works of Henry Vaughan*, 1, 57.

years. 'O! 'tis an easy thing | To write and sing; | But to write true, unfeigned verse | Is very hard!'[5] Kerplunk. There are no pony rides in his poetry, to summon up Louise Guiney's colorful image of Vaughan 'on his hardy Welsh pony, drenched in the mountain mists, close-hatted, big-cloaked, riding alone and looking abroad with those mild eyes which were a naturalist's for earth and sky, and a mystic's for the spiritual world'.[6] Vaughan's travel preference in his verse is decidedly pedestrian. He favours walking and other variant forms of bodily motion in his poetry, whether wandering, roving, running, or fleeing, and frequent recourse, as we might expect, to paths, steps, feet, sojourns, tracks, and the like. The pedestrian even animates his critical vocabulary. Herbert's followers 'had more of *fashion*, then *force*', he remarks in the Preface to the completed *Silex* in 1655. 'They aimed more at *verse*, then *perfection*.' 'Sed non passibus aequis' (but with steps that matched not his).[7] The line is from *The Aeneid*, in which the boy, Ascanius, trails behind his father. There is perhaps a note of irony here, with Vaughan looking askance at his rivals. 'Steps' recalls the title of Crashaw's *Steps to the Temple* (1646) in an idiom that also distinguishes Vaughan from his master. Herbert rarely roams. His great poetry is primarily a poetry of intricately wrapped interior spaces. Vaughan's great poems are everywhere outdoorsy, and relentlessly restless:

He knocks at all doors, strays and roams,
Nay hath not so much wit as some stones have
Which in the darkest nights point to their homes,
By some hid sense their Maker gave;
Man is the shuttle, to whose winding quest
And passage through these looms
God order'd motion, but ordain'd no rest.[8]

This is the closing stanza from 'Man', a summary poem if there ever was one about the human condition, as Vaughan understands it, but not quite the last poem in *Silex*, Part I, as we shall see.

The Vaughan I am imagining is a poet responsive on a number of levels to foot travel, in keeping with our understanding of him as a nature poet, and often measuring in verse his movement through time and space. He is always

5 *The Works of Henry Vaughan*, 2, 615.

6 Quoted from Simone Thomas, '"New Cordials, new Cathartics": Henry Vaughan the Physician' in *Henry Vaughan and the Usk Valley*, ed. Elizabeth Siberry and Robert Wilcher (Herefordshire: Logaston Press, 2016), 84.

7 *The Works of Henry Vaughan*, 2, 558.

8 *The Works of Henry Vaughan*, 1, 144.

on pilgrimage, so to speak. The poem is always in the process of unfolding its meaning on the page, before us and with us, as if reading were a shared journey on foot, as in fact it is in one of the very few poems Vaughan dedicates to describing the reading process. 'My God, when I walke in those groves | And leaves thy spirit doth still fan, | I see in each shade that there grows | An Angell talking with a man'.[9] These are the opening lines from 'Religion', in which the act of walking seems to catalyze, as if by exhalation, the spirit found in the leaves of God's two books, nature and scripture. The lines lay out the movement from topic to topic, place to place, in the manner of a casual stroll, with speaker and reader paying a visit to familiar surroundings, calling on old Biblical friends transposed from scripture into verse:

> Under a *Juniper*, some house,
> Or the cool *Mirtles* canopie,
> Others beneath an *Oakes* greene boughs,
> Or at some *fountaines* bubling Eye;
>
> Here *Jacob* dreames, and wrestles; there
> *Elias* by a Raven is fed,
> Another time by th' Angell, where
> He brings him water with his bread.

The poem will go on to challenge this ideal practice of identifying walking and reading in favour ultimately of restoring a sick land through a Eucharistic miracle that also seeks the restitution of the Eucharist as a church practice. But that hoped-for transformation happens, as it were, in a flash, at the end, whereas, it is the poem's long beginning that gives us a strong taste of what has been lost: leisurely familiarity and the pleasures of slow reading as a form of shared religious experience.

Even when Vaughan's message is to sit tight or toe the line, as happens with increasing frequency in the latter part of *Silex,* Part II, the energy or quickness in his verse often derives from the dynamic friction or tension between stasis and mobility: the ordered motion often associated with divinity, the creatures, and creation, and the restlessness of human behaviour as a consequence of the Fall and its various manifestations amid civil conflict. We can glean a simple illustration of this dynamic and how Vaughan differs from Herbert in a frequently overlooked poem of his near the end of *Silex,* Part II. 'Righteousness' is clearly inspired by Herbert's 'Constancie'. As with so many poems in *Silex*, it is created

9 *The Works of Henry Vaughan*, 1, 64.

in the manner of an answer poem, as a 'match' to use Vaughan's own word for his method of response to his 'Dear friend' Herbert in the poem 'The Match': not so much a correction of the source poem as a continuation on a different footing, or parallel track. Herbert's poem is essentially a 'definition' or 'character' poem indebted to both classical and biblical sources.[10] It poses a simple question at the outset: 'Who is the honest man?', and then offers, in seven symmetrically arranged stanzas, each beginning with the pronoun 'who' or the possessive 'whose,' the moral and social characteristics of this ideal person. Herbert's figure of constancy lives among other people. 'He that doth still and strongly good pursue, | To God, his neighbour, and himself most true'.

Vaughan re-writes Herbert's poem – almost exactly. He copies out Herbert's paratactic syntax with seven stanzas of his own, each beginning the same way, although using a different rhyme pattern, but he departs from Herbert by prefacing these with a three-quatrain proem that makes clear the shift in direction, the more concentrated and private scope of his reclusive vision.

Fair solitary path! Whose blessed shades
The old, white Prophets planted first and drest:
Leaving for us (whose goodness quickly fades,)
A shelter all the way, and bowers to rest.

Who is the man that walks in thee? who loves
Heav'ns secret solitude, those fair abodes
Where turtles build, and carelesse sparrows move
Without to morrow's evils and future loads?

The idea of the path appeals to Vaughan because it is solitary, in anticipation, in this case of 'Heav'ns secret solitude'[11], and because, as an image – a single line pointing to the invisible – it serves as a figure for all that the righteous person must exclude in this life:

Whose acts, words and pretence
Have all one sense,
One aim and end; who walks not by his sight:
Whose eyes are both put out,
And goes about
Guided by faith, not by exterior light.

10 *The English Poems of George Herbert*, ed. Helen Wilcox (Cambridge: Cambridge University Press, 2007), 262. Further references to Herbert's poetry are from this edition.

11 *The Works of Henry Vaughan*, 2, 613.

Vaughan's poem has a different kind of power from Herbert's. His line is looser, more evidently prosy, in spite of its rhyme pattern, additive in mapping out the path of righteousness, and in doing so, it produces the odd, paradoxical effect that the longer the poem runs the narrower the way seems. And the more fraught and dangerous. The final stanza reads:

> Who doth thus, and doth not
> These good deeds blot
> With bad, or with neglect; and heaps not wrath
> By secret filth, nor feeds
> Some snake, or weeds,
> Cheating himself; That man walks in this path.

Coming right after the brutally Calvinistic reference to 'secret filth', the reference to feeding 'Some snake' startles, but it is in keeping with the dark re-pastoralizing of the 'path' prompting reminiscence of a lost Eden, underscored by man's potential for now 'Cheating himself'. Perhaps, too, the image of the snake also speaks belatedly to the shift in the poem to the sinewy, serpentine shape of the stanza, coming swiftly on the heels, so to speak, of the 'Fair solitary path' of the opening quatrains? If so, the final half-line puts us back on track, with its stabilizing double deixis: '*That* man walks in *this* path' (my emphasis).

There is nothing in itself particularly surprising about a devotional poet making use of the idiom of walking. Although the figure had less appeal for other metaphysical poets with whom Vaughan is often grouped – Donne, Herbert, and Crashaw – it was a staple of religious texts and the religious life, and it acquires, in Vaughan, an ethical, moral, and psychological weight, a 'force', in his terms, often missing from the airy genre of contemporary 'walking' poems that populate the internet. The Hebrew prophet, Enoch, we know, 'walks with God'; Moses wanders in the desert; pilgrims go on pilgrimages. 'We walk by faith, not by sight' Paul remarks in 2 Corinthians 5:7, a line Vaughan quotes almost verbatim in 'Righteousness'. In a later, different key, the American Transcendentalist, Henry David Thoreau, will go on to observe in his classic essay on walking that sauntering 'is beautifully derived from "idle people who roved about the country, in the Middle Ages, and asked charity, under pretense of going *à la Sainte Terre*," to the Holy Land'.[12] Thoreau also offered a second possible etymology; that sauntering perhaps derived from the word '*sans terre*, without land or a home, which, therefore, in the good sense, will mean, having no particular home, but equally at home everywhere'. Although I do not

12 Henry David Thoreau, *Walking* (Thomaston, ME: Tilbury House Publishers, 2017), 28.

believe Vaughan ever uses the word 'saunter' in his verse, Thoreau's second version, of '*sans terre*', minus the comforting 'good sense', comports better with poems like 'Righteousness' or 'Man' than the first, associated as it is with the idea of pilgrims travelling to the Holy Land. But even this sense is not entirely foreign to Vaughan's wandering imagination.

I have in mind the poem called 'The Search', Vaughan's extravagant 95-line octosyllabic tour of the hot spots associated with the life of Christ: from his Nativity in Bethlehem to the Garden of Gethsemane, with a few side trips to places made hallow through their typological association with Jesus or by his own desert wanderings. Herbert has a poem of the same title, but if it served Vaughan at all, it was again as a point of departure. Vaughan's tour of the Holy Land is so readily and immediately visualized that a more likely source of inspiration might be either an illustrated Bible or an aide de memoire as produced, say, by Albrecht Durer in one of his woodcut series involving Christ's life and passion. But neither Herbert nor the pictorial arts captures the sense of rapid movement at the heart of Vaughan's poem, what he memorably describes at the outset as 'a roving Exstasie | To find my Saviour'.[13] In fact, Herbert, in 'The Search', characteristically eschews physical movement of any kind in favour of measuring and lamenting the spiritual distance separating the speaker from God. A Herbert poem rather more on Vaughan's mind, we discover near the end of his poem, is 'The Collar', and here the point of overlap is most interesting with regard to the manner in which Vaughan transposes the idea of 'raving', associated with madness, into 'roving', associated with movement. You will recall how Herbert's poem ends.

> But as I rav'd and grew more fierce and wilde
> At every word,
> Me thoughts I heard one calling, *Childe*:
> And I reply'd, *My Lord.*

The emergence of an interior voice, associated with God, suddenly and definitively quiets what turns out to be a child's tantrum.

It is possible Vaughan's Welsh ear was pricked by the Owen Glendowerism of Herbert's 'rav'd and grew more fierce and wilde', but 'raving' and 'roving' are analogically and sonically connected, and the twist Vaughan performs on 'raving' is to make 'roving' the central, ecstatic feature of his poem as he seeks to track his saviour. The poem is all movement and energy, the search inspiring as well as tiring, a mixture of rambling and resting, enabled, we must note, by

13 *The Works of Henry Vaughan*, 1, 66-68.

the use throughout of a frequently enjambed, rhyming tetrameter line, a device Milton had expertly used in his twin ventures into the country side, 'L'Allegro' and 'Il Penseroso'. In Vaughan's case, adjectives are shorn from the verse, lending quickness to the lines and their turns; verbs denoting motion of the mind and feet are foregrounded (and emboldened below). Driven by an overwhelming desire to find his saviour, Vaughan's 'I' passes excitedly through a biblical dreamscape a bit like a frantic tourist. He stops to ask directions to the next site, then urgently sets forth again, and along the way repeats some remarkable local (folk) lore he heard about the end of time:

I **have been**
As far as Bethlem, and **have seen**
His Inn, and Cradle; **Being** there
I **met** the *Wise-men*, **askt** them where
He **might be found**, or what starre can
Now **point him out**, grown up a Man?
To *Egypt* hence I **fled**, **ran o're**
All her parcht bosom to *Nile's* shore
Her yearly nurse; **came back**, **enquir'd**
Amongst the *Doctors*, and **desir'd**
To see the *Temple*, but **was shown**
A little dust, and for the Town
A heap of ashes, where **some sed**
A small bright sparkle **was a** bed,
Which would one day (beneath the pole,)
Awake, and then **refine** the whole.

Vaughan is not generally a comic poet in *Silex*, but there is something endearing about his enthusiastic peregrinations, his desire to walk in his master's footsteps or sit where Jesus has sat. (A fascinating modernist foil to Vaughan's dynamic travelogue, by the way, is a poem by Herbert's latter-day admirer, Elizabeth Bishop, 'Over 2,000 Illustrations and a Complete Concordance'. As the title suggests, vision, in Bishop, is weighted down by the materiality of the text, making her long at the end for the innocent sight of the child.) Vaughan's itinerary is also characteristically his. Little time is spent 'Amongst the *Doctors*' – less than a half-line; more time in the Garden of Gethsemane and Golgotha (about ten lines); and the greatest in "the Wilderness", in which Jesus undergoes the 'high temptations of hell' in the desert (Milton's subject in *Paradise Regained*), and 'With Seraphins there talked he | His father's flaming ministrie'. And then in anticipation of 'They are all gone into the world of light', the poet tells us, 'He' – Jesus – 'heav'nd their *walks*, and with his eyes | Made those wild shades a Paradise' (Vaughan's italics). This is fantastic stuff, to our eyes, and to the poet's. Vaughan's unusual use of the transitive verb 'heav'nd' is not quite a coinage. The *Oxford English Dictionary* cites several other instances contemporaneous with Vaughan, but none carries the same dazzling, imaginative force.[14] Vaughan's 'heav'nd' is the poet's means of chalking out a miraculous way for all to follow. 'Thus was the desert sanctified | To be the refuge of his bride', as if a walk, under the auspices of a visionary Jesus, just might transform the landscape into the church itself.

As is true with 'The Collar', the poet wakes from his roving ecstasy. In Vaughan's case, the fantasy is not one of clerical rebellion as it is in Herbert, in which a return to order occurs in the form of a dialogue being re-established with God. It is, rather, that the dream of Jesus' walking, and therefore of Vaughan's own desire to track His footsteps in verse, sugars 'all dangers with successe'. I take the reference to sugaring 'all dangers', in the context of the church, to be an oblique allusion to the spiritual and institutional deprivation caused by the Civil War. Moreover, in place of a firmly restored dialogue between Lord and child in Herbert, Vaughan offers something more mysterious and evocative and maybe not quite as definitive a close as Herbert's: 'Me thought I heard one singing thus'. Not God, but a ministering spirit of some sort, like Ariel from *The Tempest*, descends to offer a three-stanza corrective, of which I quote just the first. The verse dangles like a loose chain on the page, as if offering the speaker and reader a lift out of the present:

> Leave, leave, thy gadding thoughts;
> Who Pores
> and spies
> Still out of Doores
> descries
> Within them nought.

And instead of a closing response by speaker to singer, Vaughan offers a summary moral in a concluding pentameter couplet:

> Search well another world; who studies this,
> Travels in Clouds, seekes *Manna,* where none is.

14 Vaughan's strong use of the verb, in conjunction with walking and the transformative power of Jesus's eyes, can be fruitfully compared with the entries preceding it in the *OED*: Owen Felltham, *Resolves* (1628), i. xlviii. 153: 'They are idle Divines that are not heav'ned in their lives, above the un-studious man'; and S. Rutherford *Letters.* (1637; 1863) I. 225: 'Surely I were rich enough, and as well heavened as the best of them, if Christ were my heaven'.

This is itself followed by a quotation from Acts, bearing all the weight of biblical authority. Vaughan's ecstatic peregrination is definitively over.

What do we make of this closing, so different from Herbert's, and from Bishop's, in which her querying speaker yearns for a child's innocent sight? In effect, there is no clerical fold into which Vaughan can return, as there is at the end of 'The Collar'. So, Vaughan takes flight, as he often does, in something of an escapist's paradox. He rejects the apparently false allurements, a staying in the present associated with the fantasy of writing about his pleasurable journey, in favour of a transcendent inwardness that comports with his Protestantism. But – and here is where recourse to Bishop's poem is especially helpful – the turn at the end of his poem doesn't issue in a radical Protestant critique – a demystification – of the journey to the Holy Land as being idolatrous in itself. Vaughan undergoes his pilgrimage in search not of relics or shrines but of Jesus. It is ultimately misguided, not mad. In Thoreau's lexicon, 'The Search' is an idle, not an idolatrous saunter, but one that ends 'sans terre'. The image of 'a roving Extasie' lingers in our minds long after we put the poem down and move on – and perhaps in Bishop's as well.

'The Search' exhausted Vaughan's fantasy travels to the Holy Land but not his desire to perambulate in his search for divinity, as in his famous exhortation in 'Rules *and* Lessons' to

> Walk with thy fellow-creatures: note the *hush*
> And *whispers* amongst them. There's not a *Spring*,
> Or *Leafe* but hath his *Morning-hymn*; Each *Bush*
> And *Oak* doth know I *AM*.[15]

This is to take the familiar literary device of personification into new territory. Instead of merely projecting a human image onto a landscape in the manner of a pathetic fallacy, Vaughan's account of walking in the early morning 'with thy fellow-creatures' offers the opportunity to discover nature to be a living presence, continuous with the human. A walk 'with thy fellow-creatures' is a peripatetic lesson, a double awakening, one that concentrates on the separate but shared essences of God's two creations. The celebrated rabbit-or-duck phrase involving self-knowledge, 'Each Bush | And Oak doth know I *AM*,' speaks in bold caps to the recognition of a separate self-hood enjoyed by plants in a manner that would please today's ecology advocates. At the same time, the phrase shadows forth the plants' knowledge of the speaker's independent being, the familiar humanist-cum-biblical scholar's 'I *AM*.'

15 *The Works of Henry Vaughan*, 1, 99.

'*Mornings* are *Mysteries*', Vaughan will go on to say in 'Rules *and* Lessons'. They are ideal for walking and communing. More mysterious still, in their stillness, are evenings, as in the case of 'The Night', probably Vaughan's greatest poem–the poem Elizabeth Siberry reports that Seamus Heaney and Karl Miller recited on the occasion of their own pilgrimage to Vaughan's graveside in 2010, and the subject of Geoffrey Hill's brilliantly bookish essay on Vaughan.[16] 'The Night' is a fully imagined spiritual journey, whose way had been cleared by 'The Search'. In stanzas that quietly unfurl their amplitude, the poem presents not the description of a walk per se but an internal pilgrimage to the Holy Land, a silent searching flight initiated by the story in John of the first-century Pharisee Nicodemus wisely seeking Christ at night. That secretive flight is now re-lived by the civil-war speaker. Thanks in part to 'The Search', he knows that Jesus cannot be tracked among dusty artefacts of the past but is to be found alone among his 'own living works', when, Vaughan goes on to incant darkly, 'my Lord's head is fill'd with dew, and all | His locks are wet with the clear drops of night'. The poem also includes an exquisite distillation of the mysterious calling propelling the pilgrim's quest. Emerging from behind the veil of Nicodemus, the speaker asks:

O who will tell me, where
He found thee at that dead and silent hour!
What hallow'd solitary ground did bear
So rare a flower,
Within whose sacred leaves did lie
The fulness of the Deity.[17]

Lured by the vocative, our progress too is smoothed by the enjambed lines and assonantal rhymes, as we follow the questing mind unfurling in search of the unfurling leaves that, as the last line hopes, will reveal everything.

At the same time, as the closing stanzas of 'The Night' remind us, by a reverse logic walking or wandering becomes the means of measuring, of tracing, the distance between an idyllic past filled with devotional wonder and the corrupt present in which 'all things wake, and where all mix and tire | Themselves and others, [and] I consent and run | To ev'ry myre'; and nowhere more poignantly so than in 'The Retreate'. As Rebecca Solnit writes in a different context, here walking 'returns the body to its original limits'.[18] In this celebrated poem, motion seems inseparable from emotion, as if Vaughan were counting out the footsteps

16 Siberry, '"Such low & forgotten thinges": The Vaughan Heritage' in *Henry Vaughan and the Usk Valley*, 96-7; Geoffrey Hill, 'A Pharisee to Pharisees: Reflections on Vaughan's "The Night"', *English*, 38, 97-113.

17 *The Works of Henry Vaughan*, 2, 610.

18 Solnit, *Wanderlust, A History of Walking*, 29.

in his head, as he moves from a luminous remembrance of childhood, 'when yet I had not walkt above | A mile, or two, from my first love', to a present, chastened understanding of 'this place | Appointed for my second race'.[19] With the juxtaposition between walking and racing in place, the most moving portion of the poem, the greatest expression of desire, in fact, begins with the famous apostrophe summoning, through a double spondaic foot, a vision of longing, with a pun on 'long' to indicate how far Vaughan is from his goal:

> O how I long to travell back
> And tread again that ancient track!
> That I might once more reach that plaine,
> Where first I left my glorious traine,
> From when th' Inlightened spirit sees
> That shady City of Palme trees;
> But (ah!) my soul with too much stay
> Is drunk, and staggers in the way.
> Some men a forward motion love,
> But I by backward steps would move,
> And when this dust falls to the urn
> In that state I came return.

The poem has always seemed central to Vaughan's vision and oeuvre, initially because it was assumed to underlie Wordsworth's Intimations Ode with its happy memories of childhood. But Wordsworth's Ode is written in the high mode, filled with gestures of exultation in varying stanzaic forms and lengths, whereas Vaughan's poem is measurably lower in its perambulations and expectations, less demanding of applause. Like 'The Search', the lyric explores the temporal logic of tetrameter but in a slower, more melancholic mood. The full-mouthed apostrophe 'O' of longing to tread again the ancient track, we soon discover, reappears in the sound-alike personal epiphany 'ah!' over the venture's impossibility. The reduction in vocal scale prepares the way for the paradoxically splendid and startling variation on walking, in the figure of the soul drunk and staggering from too much 'stay' – in the nominal sense of staying in place or hesitating. As for the verb 'stagger', it is probably plucked from Job 12:25 ('They grope in the dark without light, and he maketh them to stagger like a drunken man').[20] Vaughan's struggles are less epical than Job's; his

19 *The Works of Henry Vaughan*, 1, 81-82.

20 For the closest sense of Vaughan's meaning, see *OED* entry for "stay," N. 3, 5a, b. Jonathan Nauman has recently found a likely source for Vaughan's drunk soul in Boethius' *Consolation of Philosophy* in Lady Philosophy's remark in 3. 2: 'In spite of its hazy memory, the human soul seeks to return to its true good; but like the drunken man who cannot find his way home, the soul no longer knows what its good is'. See p. 56 of this issue.

complaints are more plaintive. Each metrical foot forward in 'The Retreate' seems only to further Vaughan's longing to step backwards, to return to the beginning, his origins, as the poem closes quietly in on itself, in the image of dust returning to dust, and a final line that staggers slightly but quietly by being, uniquely in this poem, a half-foot short.

Although there are other inspired instances of walking – most notably in his two Ascension poems – I want to close my own ambulation by looking at one more walking poem in some detail. Many Vaughan readers, I suspect, will probably guess which it is, but in anticipation, I want to trace out a few broader issues only implicitly raised in this essay. The first has to do with what I have been calling the temporal logic of a poem. As with most Renaissance poets writing in the English language, Vaughan did not seek a mimesis or precise equation between metrical feet and subject matter. Such self-conscious attempts to make the movement of English verse mimic the subject matter did occur, of course, especially in the theatre and occasionally in courtly poems like Jonson's 'My Picture Left in Scotland', but Vaughan was generally uninterested in this punning aspect of feet. For him, movement had to do with the duration of the line and of the poem. Tetrameter especially appealed to him in these moments because of its relatively rapid turns and its applicability, therefore, to various pursuits in his poem, some forward, some backward – and in the case of the octosyllabic 'Misery', into a nearly indefinite future of depression. To borrow an idea from Geoffrey Hill and bend it in a different direction, Vaughan sensed a kind of occult sympathy or magnetism between the imaginary body's movement through space and the shape of the verse to which that experience is sometimes given expression. In this, he assimilated and reassembled the visually static element of Herbert's famous picture poems – 'The Altar' and 'Easter wings', which he never attempted to copy – into an image of quickness and mobility.

A second matter is to ask how useful a guide is Thoreau's classic essay on walking for understanding a proto-Romantic like Vaughan. For all the differences in their doxologies – 'I believe in the forest, and in the meadow, and in the night in which the corn grows', Thoreau intones[21] – the two authors obviously share a love of nature and a desire to experience nature immediately and on foot. From this angle, the most interesting perspective involves Thoreau's recurring and controversial emphasis on the concept of wildness in the wilderness. Thoreau unequivocally celebrates wildness as a manifestation of his personal and of America's westward destiny. Whenever Thoreau sets out for a walk, he adjusts his compass in a western or southwestern direction. 'Eastward I go only

21 Thoreau, *Walking*, 64.

by force; but westward I go free'.[22] And along the way, nothing attracts him more than 'a few square rods of impermeable and unfathomable bog'.[23] Wildness is also, for Thoreau, a literary value. 'In Literature it is only the wild that attracts us. Dullness is but another name for tameness'. 'English literature, from the days of the minstrels to the Lake Poets – Chaucer and Spenser and Milton, and even Shakespeare included – breathes no quite fresh and, in this sense, wild strain. It is an essentially tame and civilized literature, reflecting Greece and Rome. Her wilderness is a green wood, her wild many, a Robin Hood'.[24]

You probably see where I am going here – into the wild with Vaughan, at least part way. Further west in Wales, Vaughan doesn't quite fit into Thoreau's largely English paradigm; and yet 'wildness' is one of the features that distinguishes his poetry from Herbert's, indeed, his own often roiled religious poetry from his more classically-grounded secular verse, and one of the reasons why walking – and also walking the path – matters so much to him. The wild is something inside and outside him, a desire and a temptation, a paradox and a conflict seeking resolution, if not now, at the end of a poem, then at the end of time in God's 'deep, but dazling darkness'. As a rule, Vaughan doesn't celebrate wildness, although he urges both the north and south winds to blow on him at the end of 'Regeneration'. In fact, other than the stirrings of a quickening nature and a wish that, at the end of time body and soul will 'Rove in that mighty, and eternall light,' as he says near the end of 'Resurrection and Immortality', Vaughan, the politically disenfranchised royalist, doesn't much like wildness at all. But he also doesn't flee from it as a subject but incorporates it into his verse. That is one sign of his strength as a poet. After all, the wild, in the form of the wilderness, harboured not just people like the camel-skin-clothed, locust eating John the Baptist, whose decapitation by Salome is remembered in Vaughan's strange poem 'The Daughter of Herodias' but also Jesus.

If all this is beginning to sound a bit too gothic and scattered, let me offer a more down-to earth example, the omega to 'Regeneration's' alpha, the poem that begins 'I Walkt the other day (to spend my hour)'. Following immediately on the heels of 'Man' the opening gesture quietly initiates the body in motion, an instance of the general human condition of restlessness in that poem now being realized in the particular. If one discounts 'Begging' as an envoi, 'I Walkt the other day' is the final poem in *Silex* Part I. It couldn't have been written, furthermore, in the English tradition Thoreau recounts, not even if that tradition

22 Ibid, 52.

23 Ibid, 69.

24 Ibid, 76.

were to include, as it does, George Herbert, and even though Vaughan begins, in typical fashion, with a reminiscence of a Herbert poem, in this case 'Peace'. Herbert's poem is a decorous search for what he initially terms 'Sweet Peace'. It employs allegory in the service of a pilgrimage with various pauses along the way that include a cave, a rainbow, and a garden flower, 'The crown Imperiall'. After much wondering about some strange stalks of wheat springing from a grave, the speaker, with the help of 'a rev'rend good old man', comes to understand that peace is a product not of seeking to live sweetly but of partaking in the Eucharist, the bread of life.

Herbert's poem is an elegant lesson in typology, as neat as it is intelligible. Vaughan's poem is about airing the unintelligible. In lines that have a leisurely pace of their own to reflect the loose peregrinations of Vaughan's quest, it is a one-stop wandering descent into the underworld, an unfurling, as it turns out, in search of a rarer, less comforting flower of a different order than in 'The Night'. What is shocking and so different from Herbert, however, is not simply that Vaughan is drawn to his subject as he moves through a landscape more evidently mysterious, less allegorical, than Herbert's. It has to do with the strangeness of the encounter that digging at the base of a plant reveals. The plant harbours an unidentified grave of someone who refuses to answer the Hamlet-like speaker's intricate and rare questions, except to say, even more mysteriously than the ghost of Hamlet's father,

> that he now
> Did there repair
> Such losses as befel him in this air
> And would e'r long
> Come forth most fair and young.[25]

We, and more importantly Vaughan, do not discover the actual cause of death – sickness? slaughter? – although extorting (Vaughan's strong phrase) that information seems to have been the purpose of the questions, but apparently the 'repaired' dead person does plan to reappear again soon, 'most fair and young'. Readers are quick to see here in the projected return a symbol of the resurrection, but listen to the speaker's immediate response:

> This past, I threw the Clothes quite o'r his head,
> And stung with fear
> Of my own frailty dropped down many a tear

25 *The Works of Henry Vaughan*, 1, 144-6.

Upon his bed,
Then sighing whisper'd, *Happy are the dead*!
What peace doth now
Rock him asleep below?

Where is the comfort of the resurrection here? In place of the reassuring 'I *AM*' of 'Rules *and* Lessons', there *is* something profoundly alien, monstrous, in this landscape, not that it cannot be recuperated in the name of doctrine or lore, whether Christian or Hermetic. The speaker will soon begin to do so in the next stanza, and many scholars will follow. But the sting of fear dramatized here, the keen sense of having violated something in nature, of having restlessly looked into the 'face of things' and the self-chastening that comes from this encounter with the dead, is acute. It can only be fully resolved through what I want to call the baroque extremity, the corresponding wildness, of the final three, frame-breaking stanzas. These are the only stanzas not end-stopped in the poem. They may look like the others, but their combined effect sets them apart in a manner Vaughan must have found thrilling to plot, especially in the striding enjambments across the stanzas. Through the vehemence of prayer, the idle wandering or sauntering that produced this alien encounter is exorcised, line by line, rung by rung, as Vaughan *tracks* God's primal energy, his spirit, heavenward:

O thou! whose spirit did at first inflame
And warm the dead,
And by a sacred Incubation fed
With life this frame
Which once had neither being, forme, nor name,
Grant I may so
Thy steps track here below,

That in these Masques and shadows I may see
Thy sacred way,
And by those hid ascents climb to that day
Which breaks from thee
Who art in all things, though invisibly;
Show me thy peace,
Thy mercy, love, and ease,

And from this Care, where dreams and sorrow raign
Lead me above,
Where Light, Joy, Leisure, and true Comforts move

Without all pain,
There, hid in thee, shew me his life again
At whose dumbe urn
Thus all the year I mourn.

Robert Frost once said: 'The sentence is everything–the sentence well imagined. See the beautiful sentences in a thing like Wordsworth's To Sleep or Herrick's To Daffodils'.[26] Frost was no slouch in these matters. His Shakespearean sonnet, 'The Silken Tent', is knowingly – triumphantly – spun out of a single sentence, as he liked to acknowledge on occasion. To this list of 'beautiful sentences', I want to employ the ocular and say 'see' too the one at the end of Vaughan's 'I Walkt the other day'. Less mannered than Frost's, Vaughan's twenty-one line-sentence represents a different kind of triumph in discovering its way to its final pause. In the beginning prayer, we see in the mind's eye, a flicker of the poem's gathering quickness in the reference to the 'frame', an oblique allusion as Jonathan Nauman notes, to 'the body of the poet's brother',[27] but a self-marking as well of the poem's initial coming into being, now newly energized. Then the steady climb upward and outward in the recognition of God's omnipresence ('Thee | Who art in all things, though invisibly'), which continues in the expanded prayer heavenward for a vision of peace of 'Light, Joy, Leisure, and true comforts'. The terms are borrowed largely from Herbert's 'Heaven', the penultimate poem in *The Temple* period. They now enjoy their own metrical pacing and pressure in Vaughan's single line, set off against the phrase 'Without all pain,' a redetermination of Herbert's emphasis on "pleasure" in a Miltonic direction still registering a sense of loss. Vaughan's concluding request for revelation – 'There, hid in thee, show me his life again' – consequently takes us in a different direction than heavenward. The turn at the end returns us to the elegiac occasion, the object of mourning, in the manner of a final bow of the head and the sense of a poet true to his subject: 'At whose dumbe urn | Thus all the year I mourn'. In a brief preface fitly titled 'The Way There', Frost cryptically commented: 'footbeats for the metre and heartbeats for the rhythm'.[28] The full arc of Vaughan's long sentence settles in on itself, makes good through its final steps, the long year's temporal claim to mourning, as the walker quietly, heroically, arrives at the end of a journey that has been, as Merrill would say, 'unbeatable'.

26 Frost to Sidney Cox, 2 Feb. 1915, in *Selected Letters of Robert Frost*, ed. Lawrance Thompson (New York: Holt, Rinehart, Winston, 1964), 151.

27 Nauman, 'The truth and light of things: Henry Vaughan and Nature,' in *Henry Vaughan and the Usk Valley*, 66.

28 Frost: *Collected Poems, Prose, & Plays*, ed. Richard Poirier and Mark Richardson, New York, LOA (1995), 847.

Night Snow, Snowdon
by Colin See-Paynton

FRANCES-ANNE KING

Nautilus

after 'Nautilus' Michael Eden, 2015

Sunbeams flood
its fretwork with the force

of water,
as if to melt its solidity –

perhaps
allow its liquid form

to uncurl at night,
                    float

sodium-lit streets,
trawling for that rich, thick

juice of dreams
that pulse through shadows.

It could be
a pelagic mollusc

reinvented as a helmet
Achilles might have worn –

a present
from his sea nymph mother –
or,

the skull of some
extra- terrestrial invader,

discovered in the burning sands
of Arizona.

A real nautilus
                        swims deep,
resists great pressure;

as it grows it seals its past off
                    chamber by chamber –
never revisits it.

Lucky nautilus – or is it? –
living in the water's moment,

unable to regret,
to hear the mind's faint knocking,

its whispered words
or that creak of movement
            behind a frail partition.

It just
moves forward into larger spaces,

slowly increasing
its almost perfect spiral;

carries
nothing but its own creation,

adapts
to different waters

as it drifts those
              deep, dark slopes

of stricken coral reefs,
unfazed by fading light.

If
I could run my fingers

across this glassed-off sculpture,
roam its scrollwork

for a moment,
swim like the nautilus,
            innocent of need . . .

HOWARD WRIGHT

Clocks

All the mantel clocks have stopped at the same time,
winding down on fireplace, sideboard and shelf;

insides withered, spent, defunct. It's the dying, then death,
of each heirloom in chestnut and rosewood housings,

an unhinged family of glass and brass, that I begin to hear.
Open the flimsy backdoor, there is more space

than workings, more dust than metal. And as none has
the same mechanism, I must stoop beneath the stairs

to unhook big butterfly keys until, room by room,
the ensemble gets going again under the comfortable push

of thumb against knuckle; the out-of-kilter, ancient
twangs, clangs and pings, hammers hitting steel springs

in discord, analogue entropy as disconcerting and odd
as sudden footfalls upstairs in an empty house.

MARC HARSHMAN

Glebe Wall, Oxfordshire

Easter, 1983

And so the work goes
        on around the dead,
        orderly in its battle
        with the old chaos,
        the unpredictable,
        the stony weather.
Workers chip and scrape, fit
        the warm limestone,
        chinker it to stay, line
        the tuck-scored ribbons
        of top coverbands true,
        the lower seams already
        settling firm, foundational.

Firm in their pattern
        are a man's words to his son,
        to lay off a bit
        on the trowel, trust
        the feel of the stone, let it
        be finding its own
        place next the others.

Not easy to find your place
        in the work, the not-quite-forever,
        to make sure, as if of yourself,
        your own fit in the wall
        and its eventual passing.
This, then, the final design: to be
        from the earth, rough-worked, and plumb.

At night, the moon mixes its milk
        with these golden stones
        and they glow, raise

an aureole
around these thin, slapdash markers of the dead,
these other stones
austerely lettered
with messages about time
and the future beyond.

To such places we've come
through generations,
through rain and muck,
in shine and heat
to remember what's gone.

At noon, the workers' lime-blistered,
stiffened fingers relax and,
eyes half-closed,
backs against their yew,
they rest.

Voices circle them, schoolboys
and mothers, the vicar,
others familiar with the names
inside this mending wall,
some with admiration
for a labour they could only
know as hard
when for the men
it is only that to which
they always return.

Today, they will not
have led onto the site
much new stone.
Today, they come to re-point and score
what's already been lain, come
to score again the joints and tie-in
the bands of unwieldy rocks,
not from a quarry, not from Headington,
but detritus from a local field.

Weathered by soot, fog, and ice,
and dressed with ivy,
these honey-coloured stones lift
a wall of solid shadow
near the churchyard, a wall
held firm by intricacies
of vine, root, and the human
tally of time and heart.
These are what will withstand
the frozen-ground-swell under,
the eternal and seasonal threats.

So they will re-puzzle the old,
the gap-toothed
give-ins of rain and frost
and insidious frictions begun
somewhere in the hearting,
and with the pieces knocked out
to clear room for repair,
it will then be one over two,
two over one, batter to match
the current taper, practiced sightings
for scrap colour and shape
to line up at last
a proper coping.

In all weathers stone upon stone,
their garland once advanced beside fields
full of Suffolks and Southdowns,
beside still leas where
the numbing weight of cold
weighed even their dreams with stone.

And day upon day
the work got done,
and there were songs and
jeers, ancient riddles
and tawdry gossip,
and once when I was there,
watching, and the Isis still as glass,

pebble stones were skipped
and gaiety
lifted like echoing song
across the mead,
as yet unplanted with the dead,
and laughter rang, re-echoed,
re-pointed itself
and,
like plainsong, lifted
the long-ago into the present.

And I thought how next door
far earlier stones had been uplifted,
had lifted the church
of The Someone Famously Holy and Innocent,
that beyond this glebe wall
and between ancient yew and chestnut
a church had risen and still stands,
rose window and bell tower,
zig-zag chevrons rounding
its Norman arches, colonettes
whose master carver gave
a swallow a nest for her young.

Plain singing and bird song . . .
what more could there be
but this place to give room for
and remember calloused hands
with a feel for the work?

And in my hands this moment:
the feel of rough stone
and before me
a glimpse of one lifted away.

The italicized quotation concluding the ninth stanza is from the poem, "Mending Wall," by Robert Frost. The italicized quotation in stanza eleven is from the eighty-fourth Psalm.

PAUL CONNOLLY

Struldbrugs

Her strides are long and plosive on the treadmill,
though perhaps the headphones hurt, for the taut
inward pursings of eye and mouth
pull towards the sags that will accompany
shuffles and heaves. He counts his steps
on an app attached to his wrist, portable
radiocardiogram, hauls A&E
along for the stroll, jogs with physicians,
and notes calorie ingest and burn
in a diary with calligrapher precision, until
the nurses hold him down while another
cleans the faeces from the furniture. Massage,
irrigation, mindfulness, a single glass
of wine per day, per week, no wine,
two hundred and fifty two wanks per annum
to preserve prostate integrity, suborning
quisling bacteria to undermine their fellows,
tucks, injections, selfies in the Louvre,
instagraming the world your meals, proclaiming
yourself a hashtag crusader, the lead
in your internet comedy, problem-play
walk on, play-as-cast, or cut
in everyone else's, you embrace light's
centripetal illusion, coextend and prolong
yourself, for prolongation absorbs, and what's easier
for you than you, what fills an absence
better than yourself, and staves away
the caking nappy, the naughty, errant
clot that leaves your mouth adroop,
hearing friendly words without
a notion that they're words or friends
or children, the heath, rain and trials
of quiet, pissy scented rooms, and in the days
through many days, thought on or sensed

as animal panic in a mind's blankness,
that worse will come, and a terror that release
from worse is worst of all, yes,
applauded by the many campaigns, for extension,
universal superannuation, deferred ungratification
you'll quell a whispered *eat, drink*
and be merry for tomorrow you'll surely be alive.

London Baptism

under the railway bridge
a sudden heavy gob anointed
his hair and scalp, front centre-
right. Fifteen seconds later
it burst, bled warm from his fringe,
tip-tongued the brow, its chrism
indelible despite fingertips,
cooling aether's flight and vestige.

LAWRENCE SAIL

Sea Pictures

As a boy, when the Odeon stood in for the ocean
I saw for myself, in black and white,
just how welcoming the water could be –
how easily a body tipped up
slid from its canvas shroud with never
a murmur of a splash.

*

From the swimmer's unsteady eye level
the waves race away ahead, each crest
as it flares and flows swallowing the land,
each trough in its brief slack
allowing it to show. The deckled shoreline
comes and goes.

*

At the hour when the candle burns blue
a man is wading out, each step
more and more dogged by heaviness.
The sea resists him. He needs it to help,
to take him in, rinse him clean
of every sorrow.

*

The idea of the sea is intense light
holding above the network of hedges
in the last high field: it could be nothing else.
One final effort – the weary hoplites
clear their throats, get ready to shout
Thalassa! Thalassa!

*

The sea laps to shore like a well-trained pet,
the water clear enough to cast shadows
on its smooth ground. Or snaps a mast,
shouts at you, has the sails flogging
like pumped-up ghosts. Never look to the sea
for consistency.

On a summer night, when the salt breeze
blows steady and warm, it sometimes happens
as it twists low past riding hulls,
with the land shrunk into darkness, that the sea
will relax and throw the whole sky
wide open.

MARGARET WILMOT

Here on earth

Vedi che si trasforma questo lembo
di terra solitaria in un crogiuolo – Montale

3

The dark at the edge of the box of light is a relief.
We don't have to look, can focus on John Hurt
as he peers side-stage into what isn't there before
seating himself beneath the yellow bulb.

I think of the bundle of rags in her chair
who was my neighbour, the night she spent
failing to get a leg into the second knicker-hole.
She gave up at 6 a.m. *I'd shot my bolt.*

What tape would she choose? Krapp's banana droops.
He rewinds. Listens. Despite the gall
of life, the crap under the yellow bulb, there are
moments – they move him, move in him still.

. . .

6

We'd been going over old texts she'd translated,
this spinster of an older school, when she
broke off, stood up with sudden urgency.
Come see my goldenrod! She fairly thrust me

into the unkempt space out back. Past
the bins and dead grass poking up through cracks
in old cement, the scrubby waste was washed
with gold – and she too gilded, standing there,

glimpsing a first world again with child eyes,
it bursting on her so she had to share.
Chinks in time. *Look! Look!* I hear my own voice
tug Grandma from her cooking out the door.

THOMAS R. SMITH

Dartmoor Morning

for Sarah Delfont

The grass nibbled to a crewcut by spray-
painted sheep both sparkles and absorbs
our footsteps on its great jewelled sponge.
The early morning is quiet and vast,
rock tors rising up and wooded valleys
dipping below. The land wraps around in
folds, no beginning or end, suggesting
the eternity of nature before we came.

Cattle and sheep exchange commentary.
The ancient voice of the cuckoo adds
its tuppence-worth. A meadow
pipit runs through every song it knows.
This music springs from hill and vale
with the sparseness of the occasional
gnarly moor hawthorn that has secured
its lease with the rocks and wind.

Across the valley, a field of bluebells
smokes the green. A farm, persistent
anchorite, clings to its fold in the
decayed volcanic slope. And the rocks,
what to make of these piled slabs atilt
one another, the persistence of eons
long eroded away, or maybe
the petrified stool of giants.

Earth and water are evident. Fire must be
the yellow-burning hummocks of gorse,
the sugar-heat of blueberries building
toward a summer blossoming. Or
do the hottest flames surge through the veins

of the rangy wild ponies, the gangly
black foal learning at its mother's ragged
side the wild freedom of its kind?

On the moor it's air that gets the final
say, determines the aspect by which
we'll experience Her. Mist can make
lost, but these are simply two low-
creeping clouds rolling toward each other,
one from Hay Tor and the other opposite,
as Sarah observes, a dragon about to
devour a snake. The crocodile jaws

are wide open now, and the snake steams
into it, the white a single wall
flinging its vapors higher, starting a new
cloud-pile. The sphinx-profile of
Hay Tor becomes indistinct. We're
losing morning sun, a cooler weather
slides in. We begin threading our way back
over the moor's perfectly suspended time.

JOHN BARNIE

Nature Study

Picture the mountain beetle rolling sheep's dung,
a tiny Hercules, black as determination;

picture the hovering kestrel and the feast it makes,
extruding chitin on a fence post on the Rholben;

picture ourselves waiting for the curtain-call,
life the amateur drama group's poor little show,

wondering whether, now the play is over,
anyone will cheer as the Earth stacks the chairs.

Sunglasses

We send smileys when we're happy, boo-hoos when we're sad,
don't see the Bud can crushed at the bottom of the Marianas Trench,

where, the weirdest thing, a neon jellyfish floats, itself its own fairground,
at that depth, under that pressure; only think; but there's no emoticon for
think.

'*The Philosopher's Vision: Experiencing the Consolatio Philosophiae in Silex Scintillans and Thalia Rediviva*'

JONATHAN NAUMAN

23rd Vaughan Association Colloquium (Brecon, Wales)
April 22, 2018

Readers of Henry Vaughan's sacred verse have commonly acknowledged the important component of Christian Platonism in the visionary intimations that characterize the best-known lyrics of *Silex Scintillans*.[1] However, it is not overly common to find this aspect of the Vaughan's work specifically connected with his evident interest in Boethius's *Consolation of Philosophy*, a Platonist text of Christian authorship unrivalled in its intellectual and literary influence during the poet's time and for more than a millennium before. I would suggest that the general absence of inquiry into Boethian influences in Vaughan's sacred work has resulted largely from differences between Vaughan's working assumptions about the *Consolatio* and those held by certain of his mid-twentieth-century readers. One might take for instance Harold R. Walley's efforts to analyze and date the contents of Vaughan's unapproved *Olor Iscanus* collection.[2] In arguing that the poems and translations of that volume are "arranged in a roughly chronological order" (31), Walley observes that "the selections from Boethius,

1 See for instance Douglas Bush's appraisals in *English Literature in the Earlier Seventeenth Century, 1600-1660* (New York: Oxford University Press, 1945), p. 145: "As Herbert contains in himself two poets, the Anglican priest and the spiritual struggler, so in Vaughan there are the Herbertian religious poet and the timeless (but no less Christian) Neoplatonist." Bush observes that "it is the latter and larger Vaughan that we cherish"; however, he also perceives that practical and quotidian efforts in Christian piety as rendered in the more pedestrian testimonial verse and in the devotional prose seem to have enabled "the strength and centrality of [Vaughan's] richest intuitions of the invisible."

2 "The Strange Case of *Olor Iscanus*," *Review of English Studies* 18 (1942): 27-37. This examination remains one of the most complete assemblages of the data available for the dates and circumstances of Vaughan's original lyrics and translations in this collection.

which constitute the bulk of the translations," introduce after those from Ovid and Ausonius "a new depth and earnestness of tone," while

> the translations from Casimirus, which follow, provide a natural sequel as well as an important addition. Repeating the *contemptus mundi* of Boethius, they substitute for his Stoic virtue the love of God . . . Thus the pagan consolation of Boethius is transmuted to the Christian faith of Casimirus.[3]

F. E. Hutchinson in his standard biography of Vaughan explicitly reiterates and extends Walley's observations.

> Vaughan's passing from Ovid and Ausonius to Boethius marks the growing seriousness of his mind, and next he leaves the pagan consolation of Boethius for the Christian faith of Casimir. This contention seems justified, although Casimir's lyrics are Horatian rather than explicitly Christian.[4]

It is interesting, and indeed diagnostic, to find Hutchinson plying a similar distinction in his survey of Vaughan's *Flores Solitudinis*: "Nieremberg's *De Arte Voluntatis* (1631), from which Vaughan selected two long sections for translation, was a work intended to give the pith (*medulla*) of Platonic, Stoic, and Christian ethic, and is therefore more plentifully illustrated from pagan writers–Plato and the Platonists, Seneca and Epictetus–than from Christian."[5]

However, when Henry Vaughan translated John Nieremberg's discourses on "Temperance and Patience" and "Life and Death" for his second prose devotional volume, issued at the height of his Christian rigorism in 1654, he probably did not think of "Plato and the Platonists, Seneca and Epictetus" along the lines of Hutchinson's taxonomy as "pagan writers."[6] Rather, he took

3 *Ibid.*, p. 32.

4 *Henry Vaughan: A Life and Interpretation* (Oxford: Clarendon Press, 1947), p. 56.

5 *Ibid.*, p. 132.

6 Hutchinson must be seen here to be using "pagan" in its most general sense, analogous to "gentile" in the Jewish tradition, for "Plato and the Platonists, Seneca and Epictetus" were not particularly inclined to advocate the cultus of the Greco-Roman pantheon. One sees in the instances cited here how the progressivist latitudinarian movement in nineteenth-century Anglicanism, which Canon Hutchinson strongly supported, paradoxically tended to narrow what was admitted to the category "Christian." This resulted from latitudinarian advocacy of the emergent social sciences over against traditional creeds or Christian doctrinal statements. See Nauman, "F.E. Hutchinson, Louise Guiney, and Henry Vaughan," *Scintilla* 6 (2002): 135-147 for an account of the effects of this point-of-view on Hutchinson's Vaughan work.

them to be Philosophers, whose achievements in natural human reason anticipated and supported Christian doctrine, a position which reflected the opinion of the Jesuit author he was translating. For Henry Vaughan this point would be of some importance, because such rapprochement with classical philosophy was seen in his time as a stance distinctive to leading figures in the episcopal Anglican Counter-Reformation, a movement that the Royalist and liturgical traditionalist poet staunchly supported. William Laud, Lancelot Andrewes, and Richard Hooker resisted the idea that Christian revelation "had been given to men as a substitute for all other knowledge, including science, ethics and metaphysics"; instead, they "built up theological doctrines in which the fundamental agreement of natural and revealed knowledge was everywhere either stated or presupposed."[7] Hooker had penned an extensive and prototypical defense of this position in his *Laws of Ecclesiastical Polity*:

> There is in the world no kind of knowledge, whereby any part of truth is seen, but we justly account it precious; yea, that principal truth, in comparison whereof all other knowledge is vile, may receive from it some kind of light; whether it be that Egyptian and Chaldean wisdom mathematical, wherewith Moses and Daniel were furnished; or that natural, moral, and civil wisdom, wherein Salomon excelled all men; or that rational and oratorial wisdom of the Grecians, which the Apostle St. Paul brought from Tarsus; or that Judaical, which he learned in Jerusalem sitting at the feet of Gamaliel: to detract from the dignity thereof were to injury even God himself, who being that light which none can approach unto, hath sent out these lights whereof we are capable, even as so many sparkles resembling the bright fountain from which they rise.[8]

One notes that Hooker's expositions in support of traditional Anglicanism cited Boethius's *Consolatio* as an authority,[9] effectively endorsing an earlier Christian author who had modeled the practices Hooker was recommending. Hooker's usage certainly followed mainstream opinion of a text translated, emulated, and theologically approved by such figures as Alfred, Aquinas, Jean de

7 Etienne Gilson, *Reason and Revelation in the Middle Ages* (New York: Charles Scribner's Sons, 1938), pp. 5, 16.

8 John Keble, ed., *The Works of that learned and judicious divine Mr. Richard Hooker*, 3 vols. (New York: Burt Franklin, [1888] 1970), I: 370 (*Of the Laws of Ecclesiastical Polity*, Book III, Chapter viii, paragraph 9). All of Book III, Chapter viii in Hooker's *Ecclesiastical Polity* addresses the legitimacy and value of philosophical reasoning in the Christian tradition.

9 See Hooker's discourses on the goodness of Divine Providence (*Ecc. Pol.* I. ii. 6, *op. cit.* I:204) and on the validity of lay baptism (*Ecc. Pol.* V. lxii. 21, *op. cit.* II:302).

Meun, Dante, Chaucer, and Elizabeth I. In short, it is reasonably certain that Henry Vaughan did not consider the insights of his Boethian *metra* to be a "pagan consolation." They were, precisely, a *Consolation of Philosophy*, relaying Platonic insights fully compatible with the Christian religion, understood to be gracious gifts from the Holy Trinity through natural revelation.

Walley's and Hutchinson's academic inclinations to classify Boethius as a pagan writer seem to have resulted from a passing fashion which gained currency in the eighteenth century and considerable popularity in the nineteenth among historians of theology and philosophy. It is some testimony to delayed communications between disciplines that by the first decades of the twentieth century these theories denying that Boethius authored his theological *Tractates* and characterizing him as a pagan or lapsed Christian had already begun to lose favor among historians. For instance, the Introduction to the Loeb Classical Library volume on Boethius, written in 1926 by two scholars who had themselves formerly been caught up in the earlier speculations, reported that recent advances in scholarship had shown clearly, through both internal and external evidences, that Boethius was author both of the *Tractates* and of the *Consolatio*; that his achievements in these texts showed him to be a pioneer in Christian philosophical theology, "the last of the Roman philosophers, and the first of the scholastic theologians"; that "Boethius was without doubt a Christian, a Doctor and perhaps a martyr."[10] This understanding of Boethius as a sophisticated logician whose *Consolatio* was "an essay in natural theology apart from revelation"[11] strengthened as the twentieth century proceeded and seems to be retaining favor in the new millennium even among scholars inclined to dismiss the medieval and early modern receptions of the *Consolatio* as distortions.[12] When

10 H. F. Stewart and E. K. Rand, eds., *Boethius: The Theological Tractates; The Consolation of Philosophy* (London: William Heinemann; Cambridge, Massachusetts: Harvard University Press, [1962] 1918), pp. x-xi. For Stewart's and Rand's developing opinions about the Boethian *corpus*, see Henry Chadwick, *Boethius: The Consolations of Music, Logic, Theology, and Philosophy* (Oxford: Clarendon Press, 1981), p. 302, n. 7.

11 Chadwick, p. 251.

12 See for instance Danuta Shanzer, "Interpreting the *Consolation*" in John Marenbon, ed., *The Cambridge Companion to Boethius* (Cambridge: Cambridge University Press, 2009), pp. 228-254. Shanzer calls for a "more nuanced view of spectrums of belief and practice that leave a place for people such as Boethius [who] cannot simply be pigeon-holed under monolithic labels, such as 'Christian' or 'pagan'" (242); but she also describes her own approach to the religious affiliation of Boethius's most famous text as an effort "to get a sense not of whether or not Boethius was a Christian (for he clearly was), but of *what sort of a Christian he was*" (241, emphasis in original). Now that Boethius's contributions to Christian theology are generally recognized, scholars have moved on to consider such topics as his influence as a reader of Augustine and his efforts toward "preserving Aristotelian logic from disappearing from theology"; see Julia Dietrich, "Boethius's Reading of the "*beati Augustini scriptis*" in the *Opuscula sacra*," *Carmina Philosophiae* 21 (2012): 43-65.

Walley and Hutchinson characterized the arguments of Vaughan's Boethian *metra* as a "pagan consolation" to be left behind in Vaughan's sacred phase, they seem to have been working under assumptions not only alien to Vaughan's sensibility, but also outside the scholarly consensus of their own day and of ours.

It is then unsurprising that the Platonic thoughts and images of the *Consolatio* surface repeatedly in *Silex Scintillans*; and widespread as these images were in the seventeenth century, it seems likely in many cases that Boethius was for Vaughan their most proximate source. Take for instance the poem "Vanity of Spirit,"[13] in which Vaughan projects the persona of a natural philosopher seeking the fountainhead of the world's complexity and beauty. In the *Consolatio* Book 3, Prose 11 through Prose 12,[14] Lady Philosophy examines the dynamics of mineral, vegetable, and animal life, seeing all natural striving as effort to reach a unified good, which she finally helps Boethius identify with God (66-70). Poem 11 provides an important transition in the argument, urging the need to search one's own spirit in order to transcend the usual physical constraints on human thought life.

> The man who searches deeply for the truth, and wishes to avoid being deceived by false leads, must turn the light of his inner vision upon himself. He must guide his soaring thoughts back again and teach his spirit that it possesses hidden among its own treasures whatever it seeks outside itself.
>
> Then all that was hidden by the dark cloud of error will shine more clearly than Phoebus; for the body, with its burden of forgetfulness, cannot drive all light from his mind. The seed of truth grows deep within and is roused to life by the breath of learning. For how can you answer questions truly unless the spark of truth glows deep in your heart? If Plato's muse speaks truly, whatever is learned is a recollection of something forgotten. (69)

Vaughan's speaker in "Vanity of Spirit,"

> having passed
> Through all the creatures, came at last

13 Alan Rudrum, ed., *Henry Vaughan: The Complete Poems* (Harmondsworth, Middlesex: Penguin Books, [1983] 1976), pp. 171-172. Henceforward, quotations from Vaughan's poems will be cited parenthetically within my text to this edition.

14 Here and below, quotations in English from the *Consolatio* will be cited from Boethius, *The Consolation of Philosophy*, Richard Green, tr., Indianapolis, Indiana: Bobbs-Merrill, 1962.

> To search my self, where I did find
> Traces, and sounds of a strange kind.
> Here of this mighty spring, I found some drills,
> With echoes beaten from the eternal hills;
> Weak beams, and fires flashed to my sight,
> Like a young east, or moon-shine night. (ll. 13-20)

The speaker here is able to detect, like Boethius with the help of Lady Philosophy, some "spark of truth" in his own seeking mind, some echoes in the flows of his own consciousness indicative of its source in God's "mighty spring." The persona in "Vanity of Spirit" experientially projects Boethius's Platonic sequence of thought, ending with Vaughan's perennial aspirations toward union with God after bodily death.

> *Since in these veils my eclipsed eye*
> *May not approach thee, (for at night*
> *Who can have commerce with the light?)*
> *I'll disapparel, and to buy*
> *But one half glance, most gladly die.* (ll. 30-34)

The poem following "Vanity of Spirit" in *Silex Scintillans* is "The Retreat" (172-173), much-recognized for its Platonic resonances. Because its opening lines, "Happy those early days! when I / Shined in my Angel-infancy," are clearly reminiscent of the first lines of Vaughan's translation from the *Consolatio* Book 2, Poem 5 in *Olor Iscanus*, "Happy that first white age! when we / Lived by the earth's mere charity" (119), "The Retreat" has attracted some critical notice connecting it with Boethius.[15] The thoughts and images of the poem do in fact bear this connection out, as the poet provides a personal descant on Lady Philosophy's observation in Book 3, prose 2 that "there is naturally implanted in the minds of men the desire for the true good, even though foolish error draws them toward false goods" (43); and Vaughan seems to have found one simile used in her descriptions of this human problem especially applicable: "In spite of its hazy memory, the human soul seeks to return to its true good; but like the drunken man who cannot find his way home, the soul no longer knows what its good is" (45).

> O how I long to travel back
> And tread again that ancient track!

15 See for instance Bush, p. 144.

> That I might once more reach that plain,
> Where first I left my glorious train,
> From whence the enlightened spirit sees
> That shady city of palm trees;
> But (ah!) my soul with too much stay
> Is drunk, and staggers in the way.[16] (ll. 21-28)

Like "Vanity of Spirit," "The Retreat" concludes with Vaughan's speaker anticipating physical death, in this case seen not as a means toward enlightenment, but as the poet's return to his Creator and to an earlier purity of vision. This dynamic seems quietly to presuppose the exalted account of souls proceeding from and returning to God offered in Book 3, Poem 9 of the *Consolatio*. Boethius presents this poem, "an epitome of the first part of Plato's *Timaeus*,"[17] as a prayer sung by Lady Philosophy to God.

> You create souls and lesser living forms and, adapting them to their high flight in swift chariots, You scatter them through the earth and sky. And when they have turned again toward You, by your gracious law, You call them back like leaping flames.
>
> Grant, Oh Father, that my mind may rise to thy sacred throne. Let it see the fountain of good; let it find light, so that the clear light of my soul may fix itself in Thee. Burn off the fogs and clouds of earth and shine through in Thy splendor. For Thou art the serenity, the tranquil peace of virtuous men. The sight of Thee is beginning and end; one guide, leader, path, and goal. (60-61)

This vision, implicit paradigm for "The Retreat," seems also to have been an important antecedent for the imagery of the final stanzas of Vaughan's most famous elegy:

> O Father of eternal life, and all
> Created glories under thee!
> Resume thy spirit from this world of thrall
> Into true liberty.

16 Louis Martz finds this image of the soul's drunken confusion also in the *Phaedo*; see Louis L. Martz, ed., *Henry Vaughan: A Selection of his Finest Poems* (Oxford and New York: Oxford University Press, 1995), p. 183.

17 Boethius, p. 60, n. 14.

Either disperse these mists, which blot and fill
        My perspective (still) as they pass,
Or else remove me hence unto that hill,
        Where I shall need no glass.[18]

Similar moments of inspiration and influence connecting Vaughan's sacred poems with his readings in the *Consolatio* can be tracked elsewhere in both books of *Silex Scintillans*, with reminiscences occurring more often than not in the visionary pieces for which Vaughan is most famous. The examination of "the fearful miser on a heap of rust" in the third stanza of "The World" (l. 31, p. 227) seems to benefit from the discourse on "the gifts of Fortune" in Book 2, Prose 5[19]: "there is nothing about [riches] that can ever really be made your own, and they are vile in themselves if you look at them carefully," Lady Philosophy says. "Are riches naturally precious, or are they precious because of some virtue of yours? What is precious about them, the gold metal or the pile of money?" she asks (30-31). This critique seems to set the tone for Vaughan's ensuing homiletic spectacle, "Thousands there were as frantic as himself / And hugged each one his pelf" (ll. 36-37), and for his comments on how "The weaker sort slight, trivial wares enslave / Who think them brave" (ll. 42-43). The same passage in the *Consolatio* advises a detachment from natural beauty that probably helped to motivate the turn toward the vision of God at the end of "The Water-fall" (306-307):

> You are, of course, delighted by the beauty of the open fields. And why not, since this is a beautiful part of a very beautiful creation. In the same way we are pleased by a serene sea, we admire the sky, the stars, the sun and the moon; but do any of these things belong to you? How then can you glory in their splendor? You are not adorned with spring flowers, nor are you laden with summer fruit. When you act as though such external goods are your own, you are deluded by foolish satisfaction. Fortune can never make things yours which nature made foreign to you. No doubt the fruits of the earth are given to animals and men for their food[20]; but,

18 "They are all gone into the world of light!", ll. 33-40 (247).

19 One notes that this prose section in the *Consolatio* leads directly into the lyric "Felix nimium prior aetas" (Stewart and Rand, p. 204) which, as mentioned above, Vaughan translated in *Olor Iscanus* and echoed in "The Retreat."

20 See *Genesis* 1: 29-30. This is one example of a number of brief allusions to Christian doctrines and to the Judeo-Christian Scriptures that constitute part of the internal evidences for the artificial rather than activist nature of Boethius's general exclusion of supernatural revelation from the *Consolatio*.

> if you simply wish to satisfy the demands of nature, there is no reason why you should struggle for the superfluities of Fortune. (31)

After a carefully perceptive and analogical appreciation of a local cascade, Vaughan ends his beautiful depictions by turning away from the waterfall in order to worship God.

> O my invisible estate,
> My glorious liberty,[21] still late!
> Thou art the channel my soul seeks,
> Not this with cataracts and creeks. (ll. 37-40)

The visionary response to nature for which Vaughan's sacred verse is rightly much noted proceeded within the context of a glad acceptance of the Platonic insights offered in Boethius's *Consolatio*, a work that Vaughan seems to have appreciated, probably quite accurately, as the natural philosophy of a classicist Christian.

If these accounts correctly suggest that Vaughan's experience of Boethius's *Consolatio* provided a significant and proximate guide for the Platonic strain in his sacred verse,[22] the appearance in *Thalia Rediviva* (1678) of five translations from the *Consolatio metra* takes on additional importance, testifying to almost continuous Boethian interests[23] throughout Vaughan's literary career. The poet's

21 Rudrum and Martz note here a reference to *Romans* 8:19, a scriptural passage Vaughan also uses in the epigraph to "And do they so?" (188-189) to argue that the souls of all creatures seek God as they are able. Vaughan's speaker's final refusal to rest in the spectacle of beautiful natural scenery in "The Water-fall" is actually an emulation of the insights the waterfall has taught him.

22 More examples could be added, including an image of theological discord in "White Sunday," "And on Christ's coat pin all their shreds" (l. 14, p. 248) likely deriving from the shredding of Lady Philosophy's robe by post-Platonic schools of philosophy in Book 1, Prose 3 of the *Consolatio* (7-8); for this connection, it is interesting to note that the best-known English translation of the *Consolatio* in the mid-seventeenth century(1609, translated by "I.T.") renders Boethius's "pro sua quisque parte" as "every one for his own sect" (Stewart and Rand, pp. 138-139). See also Boethius's descriptions of ascent to the vision of God in Book 4, Prose 1 and Poem 1 of the *Consolatio*, which seem likely to have combined with the first lines of George Herbert's "Whitsunday" to produce the initial prayer in stanza four of Vaughan's "Disorder and Frailty" (ll. 46-49, p. 203).

23 I have not detected any Boethian allusions or reminiscences in Vaughan's earliest volume, *Poems* (1646), but it may be worth noting that one of the poets most influential in Vaughan's first-published work, Thomas Randolph, performed an aesthetic burlesque on the *Consolatio* in his poem "On the inestimable content he inioyes in the muses"; see John Jay Parry, ed., *The Poems and Amyntas of Thomas Randolph* (New Haven, Connecticut: Yale University Press, 1917), p. 183. This poem of Randolph's seems to have influenced Vaughan's early poem "In Amicum Foeneratorem" (74-75).

last published verse collection has not elicited much critical praise, having been termed "an inferior volume of verse,"[24] "an after-gleaning of poems which might have found a place" in earlier publications,[25] "a repository for Vaughan's literary flotsam"[26]; however, the five Boethian *metra* in *Thalia Rediviva* do not to me manifest any decline from the poetic translations printed in Vaughan's earlier devotional and non-devotional volumes. The lyrics lack the close ordering and joint Royalist motivation of the *Consolatio* translations in *Olor Iscanus*,[27] but they do show the personal, timely, and sympathetic amplifications that Vaughan habitually practiced as a translator; and I would venture to guess that they were written sometime after the earlier-published *metra*, perhaps during the Protectorate.[28] Readings from *Thalia Rediviva* can be difficult to frame, as the collection seems to have had to be revamped by the poet's younger friends in order to get it into print,[29] making it unclear what role Vaughan himself played in choosing or ordering the poems finally included in this memorial volume for his twin brother. But it is reasonably certain that Vaughan wanted the five additional *Consolatio metra* to be printed, and his choices in translating do show clear and personal appreciation for Boethius's vision.[30]

The first of the five *Consolatio* selections in *Thalia* translates the Third Book's concluding poem, in which Lady Philosophy urges Boethius's persona, her pupil, toward resolute pursuit of truth and good through an allegorical

---

24 Bush, p. 144.

25 Hutchinson, p. 217.

26 Jonathan Post, *Henry Vaughan: The Unfolding Vision* (Princeton, New Jersey: Princeton University Press, 1982), p. 213.

27 For a survey of the Royalist inflections present in the thirteen *Consolatio metra* translations of *Olor Iscanus*, see Jonathan Nauman, "Boethius and Henry Vaughan" in Donald R. Dickson and Holly Faith Nelson, eds., *Of Paradise and Light: Essays on Henry Vaughan and John Milton in Honor of Alan Rudrum* (Newark, Delaware: University of Delaware Press, 2004), pp. 192-201.

28 Hutchinson's states that "all of the verse translations appearing in *Thalia Rediviva* were probably written by 1651" (84), but he does not specify his grounds for this, and probably his inclusion of the *Consolatio* translations in the estimate was connected with classifying Boethius's arguments as a "pagan consolation." The interpolation I note below addressing blood circulation in Vaughan's translation of Book 4, Poem 6 (p. 358, ll. 68-70) would seem to reflect developing medical interests, which bibliographical evidence especially associates with the mid-1650s.

29 See Jonathan Nauman, "The Publication of *Thalia Rediviva*," *Huntington Library Quarterly* 61 (1999): 81-91 for a discussion of this aspect of Vaughan's last publication.

30 It is possible that Vaughan's translations from Boethius in *Thalia Rediviva* helped to encourage his volume's dedicatee Henry Somerset, Earl of Worcester (later Duke of Beaufort) to pursue a full translation of the *Consolatio* several years later; see Kenneth Hawley, "Henry Somerset and his Translation of Boethius's *Consolation of Philosophy*," *Carmina Philosophiae* 19 (2010): 69-81 and Kenneth C. Hawley, ed., *Boethius's* Comforts and Consolations of Philosophy, *Henry Somerset, Duke of Beaufort, 1693*, British Library, Additional MS 40693B (printed as a special issue of *Carmina Philosophiae*, vol. 20 [2011]).

presentation of the story of Orpheus. Lady Philosophy's argument especially indicates perseverance and focus, the need to have God's light constantly in view to receive transcendent truth. Vaughan chooses in his rendering to highlight especially the danger of overvaluing the secondary good of conjugal love, emphasizing this aspect of the Orpheus tale by introducing the couple as "kind *Orpheus*" and "loved *Eurydice*" (ll. 6-7, p. 353) where the original uses neither the adjectives nor the couple's proper names.[31] The innovation is fetched up again at the story's end: where the original briefly recounts that "as they approached the edge of night, Orpheus looked back at Eurydice, lost her, and died" (74), Vaughan elaborates on the tragedy of Orpheus's misplaced priorities, focusing on the irony of following the dictates of love to the point of destroying one's lover.

> Poor *Orpheus* almost in the light
> Lost his dear love for one short sight;
> And by those eyes, which love did guide,
> What he most loved unkindly died.[32]

Vaughan's two introduced adjectives, "kind" and "loved," are interpolated once more in the summary line, "What he most loved unkindly died," migrating the emphasis away from Lady Philosophy's use of the story to advocate reasonable singlemindedness and taking it toward a point made earlier in the *Consolatio*, where Lady Philosophy affirms the reality of secondary goods while maintaining the need to subordinate them accurately to the unified Primary Good.[33] This change in emphasis can also be seen in Vaughan's choice to characterize Orpheus's backward glance not as an experience of being "conquered" and turning "his eyes to the pit of hell" (74), but as a seduction, a fatal lapse in favor of earthly goods.

> For if, while you strive to ascend,
> You droop, and towards earth once bend
> Your seduced eyes, down you will fall
> Ev'n while you look, and forfeit all. (ll. 81-84, p. 355)

31 In the *Consolatio*, Orpheus is "Vates Threicus" and Euridice is "coniugis" (see Stewart and Rand, p. 294, ll. 5-6). Boethius saves the proper names for the climax of the poem: "Orpheus Eurydicen suam / Vidit, perdidit, occidit" (ll. 50-51, p. 296).

32 One notes here that in the *Consolatio* Eurydice is "lost" and Orpheus "died." Vaughan sharpens the irony, both by highlighting the effect of Orpheus's love-obsessed mistake on his loved one, and by emphasizing the real dignity and power of conjugal love with interpolations at ll. 32-33 and ll. 71-72.

33 See Book 3, Prose 2, pp. 43-45.

The second selection from the *Consolatio metra* in *Thalia Rediviva* is a rendering of Book 3, Poem 2, a lyric that directly follows Lady Philosophy's discourse on the real power of secondary goods as motivators in human life, often causing souls to become confused, drunk "with too much stay." Here Vaughan follows Boethius closely in describing the tendencies of captured animals, the chained lions and the caged birds, to revert to their natural state, and in recounting the predictable upward growth of plant life and the prescribed path of the sun, adding little more by way of interpolation than a gesture characterizing Nature's ruling powers as forms of magnetism (l. 2)[34] and a glance at the lion-tamer "dulled with fear" as the animal he thought he had mastered attacks (ll. 19-20). But as Robert Allen Durr has noticed,[35] the final lines of this translation articulate clearly the Platonic ethos of procession and return that provided the basis for Vaughan's ring motif in "The World" and elsewhere.

Thus all things long for their first state,
And gladly to't return, though late.
Nor is there here to any thing
A *course* allowed, but in a *ring*;
Which, where it first *began*, must *end*:
And to that *point* directly tend. (ll. 43-48, p. 356)

Durr also cites the final lines of the third Boethian translation in *Thalia Rediviva*, from Book 4, Poem 6, where we find clarified again "that ancient track" sought in "The Retreat."[36]

This is the *cause* why every living
Creature affects an *endless being*.
A *grain* of this bright *love* each thing
Had given at first by their great King;
And still they creep (drawn on by this:)
And look back towards their *first bliss*.
For otherwise, it is most sure

34 Rudrum notes Vaughan's "particular affection for the metaphor of the magnet" (673). Here and elsewhere, Rudrum's notes to *Henry Vaughan: The Complete Poems* have been helpful in my tracking of Vaughan's departures from and elaborations on the *Consolatio*. L. C. Martin's notes to *The Works of Henry Vaughan*, 2nd ed., Oxford: Clarendon Press, 1957, often relayed in Rudrum's edition, have also been helpful.

35 R. A. Durr, *On the Mystical Poetry of Henry Vaughan* (Cambridge, Massachusetts: Harvard University Press, 1962), p. 41.

36 Rudrum, p. 674.

Nothing that liveth could *endure*:
Unless its love turned retrograde
Sought that *first life*, which all things made. (ll. 71-80, p. 358)

In the *Consolatio* this poem follows a prose passage containing Lady Philosophy's explanations for why all fortunes experienced in the world are actually good, an insight that Vaughan emphatically endorsed in his preface "To the Reader" in *Flores Solitudinis*.[37] The poet's rendering here features a greater variety of interpolations and elaborations than any other Boethian *metrum* he published: a reference to blood circulation indicating his developing medical interests (ll. 68-70), amplifications on the behaviors of the four elements (ll. 29-34), added observations on the natural cycles of the seasons (ll. 35-53), a moral aside on the benefits of mortality for mankind (ll. 60-62), a brief reference to astrology (l. 6),[38] and, in the quotation given above, a redescription of "the common bond of love by which all things seek to be held to the goal of good" (97) as a supernatural hermetic seed or "grain."

The fourth translated *metrum* included in *Thalia Rediviva*, Book 4, Poem 3, is a rendering of Lady Philosophy's thoughts on an episode from the *Odyssey*, the transformations inflicted on the hero's crew at the isle of Circe. In the *Consolatio* the poem follows on a prose argument maintaining that "just as virtue is the reward of virtuous men, so wickedness itself is the punishment of the wicked" (82), and the poem is meant to reinforce one's apprehension of mankind's definitive inner reality. Vaughan's elaborations here consist mainly in adding details known from other sources to the Boethian account of Ulysses's company's adventure. The poet is at his best while rendering Lady Philosophy's appraisal of Circe's failure to change the human self-consciousness of her victims.

O worthless *herbs*, and weaker *arts*
To change their *limbs*, but not their *hearts*!
Man's *life* and *vigour* keep within,
Lodged in the *centre*, not the *skin*.
Those piercing charms and poisons, which
His *inward parts* taint and bewitch,

37 Martin, p. 217.

38 Vaughan's translation changes Lady Philosophy's observation that "the war of discord is excluded from the bounds of heaven" (97) to an assertion that the stars "show our wars." This seems to indicate that he affirmed astrology as veridical even though he questions the wisdom of those who practice it in ll. 25-28 of "The Constellation" (231).

More fatal are, than such, which can
Outwardly only spoil the man.
Those change his *shape* and make it foul;
But these deform and kill his soul. (ll. 27-36, p. 359)

The fifth and last Boethian translation in *Thalia* is Book 3, Poem 6, the shortest of the set; and it could have been even shorter if Vaughan had not chosen to elaborate considerably on the nine-line Latin original in which Lady Philosophy dispatches any notion of moral value in the possessing of noble descent. After fairly close rendering of his original's statements on God being Father of all creation, Vaughan reinforces humanity's uniform status as "a noble offspring" (l. 13) with a glance toward St. Paul.

But *men* (made to inherit all,)
His *own sons* he was pleased to call,
And that they might be so indeed,
He gave them *souls* of divine seed. (ll. 9-12, p. 360)

For Lady Philosophy's simple query "Quid genus et proauos strepitis?"[39], "Why then boast of your ancestors?" (53), Vaughan supplies four lines:

O why so vainly do some boast
Their *birth* and *blood*, and a great *host*
Of ancestors, whose *coats* and *crests*
Are some ravenous *birds* or *beasts*? (ll. 15-18, p. 360)

But after this considerable expansion,[40] the strong tetrameter couplets closing the poem present Lady Philosophy's final statements on the topic quite straightforwardly and concisely.

No man, though of the meanest state
Is *base*, or can *degenerate*;
Unless to *vice* and *lewdness* bent
He leaves and *taints* his true *descent*. (ll. 21-24, p. 360)

39 Stewart and Rand, p. 250.

40 The strong interpolated rejection of aristocratic coats-of-arms might be seen to sort oddly with the presence of the poet's family arms on his tombstone in Llansantffraed churchyard. However, the words testifying to the poet's desires for his grave marker ("quod sepulchrum voluit") are inserted as an introduction to penitential Latin texts on the lower part of the stone and seem to distinguish those words from details on the stone's upper section where the arms appear.

The renderings from Boethius's *Consolatio* in *Thalia Rediviva* demonstrate Vaughan's continuing commitment at the end of his literary career to the insights and vision of Christian Platonism. I would suggest that they help reinforce an impression of Boethius's *Consolatio* being for Vaughan's sensibility something of a keystone, uniting the Latin classicism of his early poetic efforts and training with the devotional and patristic literary visions of Herbert and Paulinus. Boethius's enabling presence, almost from beginning to end of Vaughan's oeuvre, needs to be noticed more, however the continuing historical discussions of Boethius's role in ancient and medieval thought may turn.

Gaggle of Geese
by Colin See-Paynton

NEIL CURRY

Of The Puritan Dead

I

. . . a small, scarce discernible cloud,
no bigger than a man's hand,
arose in the north, which was shortly after
attended with such a storm
that never gave over raging till it had shaken,
and even rooted up, the greatest
and tallest cedars of our three nations.

II

There were the usual atrocities,
violations and mutilations;
some indeed quite 'barbarously exquisite'.

III

They went smashing
all the stained-glass windows
and stamping them into splinters:
their own ur-*kristalnacht*.

Statues of saints were knocked
from their niches,
had their heads chopped off.
'As above, so below,' it would be
soon enough.

IV

It is impossible to avoid
the doing of some very unhandsome things
in time of war.

V

One bright,
wind-worried sort of a morning
whole families of settlers
were herded onto the bridge
at Portadown and then
pushed and thrown
into the freezing waters.

Those who tried to clamber out
were either clubbed or shot.

But there was no sin in it.

VI

The past cannot be reclaimed,
but in its 'strange likeness'
must not be forgotten:
the impulses of violence, power and paranoia.

VII

It was not total barbarity:
when Oxford was taken
Fairfax set a guard
around the Bodleian.

VIII

They have cast down
the roof of the Cathedral,
taken away the five great bells
and all the doors so that hogs
come in now and root there.

IX

Had you lent an ear in the morning
or especially at even, and heard
in the tents the sound of some
singing psalms, some praying,
and some reading from the scriptures,
it would have so refreshed your heart.

X

. . . in our army we may have the sins
of men (eating and drinking)
but in yours you have those of the devil –
spiritual pride and rebellion.

XI

In that bitter cold men huddled
in the lea of corpses, too drained
to leave the field, or ward off
the plunderers who swarmed in
to strip and rob the dead and dying.

XII

To Colonel Valentine:
Sir,
    God hath taken your eldest son
by a cannon-shot. It broke his leg
and we were necessitated
to cut it away, whereof he died,
and now abideth in that happiness
we all pant after and live for.

XIII

The Interregnum:
    a gap, a lacuna,
    an aberration.

XIV

Suspected of invincibility
he was,
until death disproved it,
throwing down the zealot
who had overthrown the tyrant.

it was a waxen effigy they followed,
Marvell, Milton, Dryden et al.,
an image that they mourned for,
the reality having exploded
in filth several days beforehand.

XV

'Turn, turn your eyes to the immoderate past'

MIKE JENKINS

Another Country

for Teris Vlacos

The orange segment
of the moon
falls rapidly
down into sea
beyond our vision.

All day we've seen
another country
a stretch of water away ;
a funnel of smoke
rising mysteriously.

Its bare mountains
and forbidding stories
following us on roads
in and out of vision.
One day the ferryman . . .

It's a craggy steep neighbour,
a face apparently
without the swaying spires
of cypress trees,
soft green of olives.

Who pays the ferryman
and will he carry us over?
This harsh neighbour
has swallowed the moon.
Still, one day we'll go there.

Shapes in Bronze

for Nikos Michalopoulos

The desire for flesh
not to crack like bark or sag
with heaviness of age,
bag of regrets hauled up impossible inclines.

The desire to be fish again
in the fluid sac
of a half-moon cove,
to swim onto scorching sand.

The desire to be house-martins
cupped in a nest
in the raftered taverna,
supping the feed of air.

Artefacts for future museums
where each of us will sit,
single holes in our heads
where the wind once whistled.

PAUL MURPHY

Berlin

I could feel the chilliest wind
Under the bridges retarded by steel
& by memories. I could see
The tower lights winking on
& off. The camera lens,
A walking, talking camera – Berlin.

This is the end
Of the air bridge as lights
On the Platz blink
In the slate grey rain
That falls on a chunk
Of bricks and metal.

There's a whole list
Of favourite whores
In between the gathering day.
Berlin is going to Hell
I can hear the crackling fires
Consume it. I can hear

The throbbing jungle beat
When the city wakes
In the dawn dreaming or
The hollowed-out thrum
Of grinding tyres and metal
The new Babylon built.

I can hear the explicit
Cries of discrete people
That are everywhere.
Moony cult suburban
Scientologists, dressed up
As werewolves, a hooker

In ermine, with an L.Ron
Hubbard clause that says,
Everyone will be fired
Then instantly re-hired.
Signing on the dotted line.
The road into Babelsberg

Like a Spandau suspension
When big yellowy eyes gleam
In a dark blue-black stream
Of seeming happening things.
Ties with suits attached
Beat up the flaneur

Deposit his remains
In the Landwehr canal.
At the Siegsäule
I am standing on the heels
Of an angel, a golden angel
Who sees but cannot intervene.

Somma Vesuviana

The long elongated toe
Of the volcano is piled
On top of a million
Mosaiced pavements where

Bird, fire and stone
Crunch together.
Their shadows pound
The leadened caldera.

Beneath the tiled piety
Byzantine emptiness exudes
A star, a tree, a gorgon's mask
Poking its tongue out Janus-like

At the past and the future.

S. A. LEAVESLEY

A Countryside Town

i

A fossil on the map:
black lines ridge and curve
the thin white page.

Churchbank, Cockford Hall,
Lower Rockhill . . . Paper rustles
in our guide's hands.

Not like autumn leaves
in winged flight but as a mistress
whispers to her lover.

ii

Beneath the castle mound's crown
of stone ruins, a scattering of shops
boasts antiques and new ceramics.

Shuttered, a real ironmonger's store,
its door deadlocked closed.

iii

Every morning an old man sweeps
the valley rain from narrow streets,

then shovels barrowloads of sun
farmed from the glistening hills.

The iron nails that sole his boots
clatter against the grey pavements.

At night, he downs his Pale Ale in one.

iv

All roads lead away. The town's broken-
backed bridge can't slow the speed
of young folks in their revved cars,
disappearing;
the old man wipes
the slipstream from his lips,
and smiles.

The Lamp Post

Each time I pass, a new bunch
of lilies clamped tight
against the rushing traffic.

Autumn shrinks the verge. Petals
yellow faster. A plastic bottle
tacked up as makeshift vase

spills over with dirtied rain.
Each time I pass, my mind
relives a stranger's slip

of foot, or thought . . .
Meanwhile, roadside bindweed
creeps closer to reclamation.

One hundred and fifty thousand lamp posts
in the county,
and, on each passing,

this the only one
that still refuses to light.

GREVEL LINDOP

In Arcadia

On marble steps, under the bas-relief
of Poussin's *Et in Arcadia Ego*,
a clutch of pellets leaking steel-blue-black
shards, like fragments of those dip-in pens
          we had at my first school.

Someone's put an army of tiny warriors
through a mincer: little breastplates, helmets,
glinting dented panels, all compacted
as if by a car-crusher. How many beetles
          it takes to feed an owl!

And nearby, among crusted target-splats
of droppings, a trembling grey-and-brown-barred feather
which I pick up. A single slant cut
would make a perfect miniature quill pen;
          if only I had the skill.

Snails

Clustered higgledy-piggledy, a snug
family of newel-post knobs, fat spirals
textured with a grain like old oak or the crackled
half-polish of much-fingered book-leather,
they huddle, chocolate-tabby nuts hoarded
in a crack under the garden wall's capstone.

Each helix minutely knurled, they could be
some Victorian chess player's expensive
pieces forgotten in a cigar-box
at the back of the curio shop. But they're alive:
packed in oak leaves, sealed with a crisp
pane of gum, they've posted themselves

as rotund parcels to a future spring
which, as this pale sun creeps over their brickwork,
may have arrived today. And they've come further,
more slowly than we think, to climb this wall.
Look where an empty shell twirls, weightless,
on a spider-thread in the ivy. Place it carefully,

if you dare, at your ear. Listen: that faint susurrus
quivering through the snailbone in your head
(geometric twin to the one you hold) isn't
wind in the trees. Rather, it's the sighing
of an ocean sixty million years old.

The Allgreave Menhir

For Earl Livings

Lean on it, catch your breath. Though it was moved,
they say, some time last century, it seems right
for this bear-sized hunk of red sandstone
(just downhill from Burnt House Farm)
to face south, drinking the heat and light
that bloom these afternoons of late autumn.
You might feel four thousand years of human
existence seethe in the stone, and under it
those ages of geology. But your welcome
came when you reached around that broken
corner, into a shallow recess grooved
in the flank, and found it a perfect fit.
The fingers. The curved hollow for your thumb. That
moment, much more than your hand was taken.

EMMA LEE

Stitching America

(for Gloria)

It started at Kansas, roughly centre,
and two strands of blue for back stitches:
the calm, smooth line of a river.

At each stitch, it felt as if she was by my side
instead of undergoing another round of treatment.
Her remission had been short-lived.

The map spread north from Wichita to the Canadian border
and west to Seattle and south to San Francisco, grew major cities
and landmarks: Mount Rushmore, the Golden Gate Bridge.

They triggered memories of holidays,
healthy times exploring new places and textures.
Recollections increasing as the stitches did.

Lake Michigan bloomed in two shades of blue as the map stretched
to the eastern seaboard then south to Florida, back across Texas.
Each cross-stitch neatly railroaded. Los Angeles the final city.

When I look at it, I see her welcoming smile.
I sent pictures of the work in progress.
Sharing urged me to finish so I could show her.

On a trip in the pine-scented valley of Yosemite
I watched two mule deer fawns thread through
the tall grass as their mother watched the setting sun.

I never found out what she thought of the map.
When I think of her, I see the bustle of Cannery Row
and feel the warmth and expanse of Monterey Bay.

BRUCE MCRAE

The Day That Was Night

The day everything went missing.
A Van Gogh sky. Musical silences.
The roll call of the fallen lambs.

A day for shoveling shadows into a hole,
for winnowing cloudy constellations.
The day that was night that was day.
That smelt like popcorn and tasted of remiss.
A day for wearing cowboy shirts –
those leathery tassels, those wagonwheel stitches!

It was a quiet morning, if somewhat winsome.
The forecast was blue, with a chance of good fortune.
I remember how the birds sang backwards.
I remember the milk truck gone over the curb.
When the light fell down and cathedral's door flew open.
Great was its majesty within and loss of tradition.
Swing low! the choir chimed aloud.
And the planets faltered.

Henry Vaughan remembered: some further reflections from nineteenth century Wales

ELIZABETH SIBERRY

In the Preface to his edition of the works of Henry Vaughan published in 1871, the Revd Alexander Grosart, from Blackburn, Lancashire, lamented that Welshmen knew nothing about their fellow countryman and, of course, it took a visit in 1895 by the indomitable Bostonian scholar, Louise Guiney, to initiate a campaign to restore the poet's grave at Llansantffraed. It is, however, now possible, using, in particular local and national newspapers (www.welshnewspapersonline), to identify a group of Vaughan enthusiasts, not just in the Brecon area, but elsewhere in Wales and the wider Welsh community, who sought to bring his work to a wider audience during the nineteenth century.

Grosart wrote that he had met with:

> Welshmen in crass ignorance of really great thoughted fellow countrymen like Henry Vaughan . . . I venture to appeal to modern Welshmen to give up the nonsense of ever praising so-called Welsh 'bards' who have not left one line that lives on in universal literature and pay deserved homage to such a man as Henry Vaughan.[1]

He added that there had been more subscribers to his edition from Scotland, America and Germany than from all of Wales and that he:

> actually found a Welsh church dignitary (a native too) imagining that Henry Vaughan was some lately deceased clergyman and that his friends ought themselves to publish any collection of his works, if they deserved publication.[2]

1 Revd Alexander Grosart, *The Works in Verse and Prose Complete of Henry Vaughan Silurist*, The Fuller Worthies Library, 4 vols. (Blackburn, 1871) iv, pp. 342-3.

2 This was probably a confusion with the Revd Henry Vaughan, also descended from the Vaughans of Tretower, who was Vicar of Crickhowell from 1832-6 and whose friends published a Memoir of his Life after his death in 1837. This Vaughan also published a collection of sermons in 1833.

In 1885, perhaps prompted by the rebuilding of the church at Llansantffraed, Grosart had tried to raise interest in a 'modest monument' to Vaughan, either at Llansantffraed or Jesus College, Oxford, in the form of a memorial window and used his influence to garner support from literary figures such as Lord Tennyson, Algernon Swinburne and Robert Browning. Lack of local interest, however, meant that nothing came of this scheme, although a letter from Tennyson to Grosart confirms his willingness to participate in 'your Committee'.[3]

Grosart did, however, note that the present incumbent of Llansantffraed, Revd Thomas Watkins, 'made every possible enquiry for me with creditable interest in the fame of the poet'.[4] And he also thanked Joseph Joseph, a local antiquarian and Fellow of the Society of Antiquaries, for his help in producing his edition. Joseph, a banker, local magistrate and Mayor of Brecon from 1861-2, is known to have had a significant collection of books and manuscripts relating to Welsh history and literature, including the papers of the Breconshire historian Theophilus Jones and editions of Vaughan's poems, which he allowed other writers to use[5] and Grosart sent him a copy of his own edition of Vaughan's works, which is now in the collection of the National Library of Wales (NLW) in Aberystwyth, with the inscription 'with best regards from the editor 20 April 1871'.[6]

Grosart's notes and introduction suggest that he visited the Usk Valley as part of his research and he employed a local photographer, Thomas Griffiths of Brecon, to take photographs of the area, as illustrations for a limited edition of 50 copies. The original prints were then destroyed but the photographs selected for the edition include one of Vaughan's grave, which is significant because it shows the slab in an upright position, rather than horizontal as it is now and was when Louise Guiney first saw it in 1895. There is no indication however that Vaughan's grave was a site of literary pilgrimage. And even Joseph Joseph, who organized tours for the Brecon meetings of the Cambrian Archaeological Association in 1853 and 1872, did not include Llansantffraed on his itinerary.

Grosart's limited edition had two other Welsh subscribers- Revd. J. D. Williams of Christ's College, Brecon and the Bishop of St. David's (Brecon was part of

3 Cecil Y. Lang and Edgar F. Shannon, eds. *The Letters of Alfred Lord Tennyson*, 3 vols (Oxford: Clarendon Press, 1990), iii, p. 321 n.3. See also Grosart's response to Guiney's letter to *The Athenaeum*, 30 November 1895, p. 756.

4 Grosart, i, p. xxxiv.

5 Joseph died in 1890 and is buried in Brecon. Thomas Nicholas wrote in his *Annals and Antiquities of the Counties and County Families of Wales,* 2 vols (London: Longmans, 1872) i, pp. 116-77, that Joseph 'gathers these treasures not for concealment, but for use.'

6 Joseph's collection, known as the Castell Gorfod collection (NLW GB 0210 Casfod) because Joseph's daughter had married into the Buckley family in Carmarthenshire, also included original editions of Vaughan's works.

this diocese at this period). A couple of other photographs were attributed to Miss Cooke, who lived at Shellesley Kings, Worcester but was a descendant of the Picards who had owned Scethrog Tower, so that family seems to have retained an interest both in the area and Vaughan.[7]

Grosart's complaint about Welsh indifference is supported by the relatively few references to Henry Vaughan in accounts written by travellers and more general guides to the history and geography of Breconshire and Wales. Thus, Benjamin Heath Malkin seems unaware of the Silurist in his *Scenery, Antiquities and Biography of South Wales* published in 1807 and in 1833, Samuel Lewis devoted more words in his *Topographical Dictionary of Wales* to Thomas Vaughan, 'a respectable Latin and English poet', than Henry, 'author of *Olor Iscanus* and several other poems'.[8] Neither twin merited a mention in George Nicholson's *Cambrian Traveller's Guide* published in 1840. Thomas Nicholas, who drew heavily on Joseph's collection of books and manuscripts, however, did include 'the rare old poet Henry Vaughan Silurist', as one of those most 'worthy of mention' in his 'Note on Remarkable Men of Breconshire'.[9]

A similarly patchy record can be found in nineteenth Welsh biographical dictionaries. In his *Biographical Dictionary of Eminent Welshmen (Enwogion Cymru)*, published in 1852, when he was Vicar of Llangadwaladr in Denbighshire, the Revd. Robert Williams provides quite detailed entries for both Henry and Thomas Vaughan, listing their works and quoting as his sources Anthony Wood, author of *Athenae Oxoniensis* and Theophilus Jones.[10] But John H Parry's *Cambrian Plutarch Comprising Memoirs of some of the most Eminent Welshmen,* published in 1834, makes no mention of the Vaughans and they also do not feature in two early 20th century dictionaries by Revd. T Mardy Rees -*Notable Welshmen, 1700-1900,* published in 1908 and T. R. Roberts's *Eminent Welshmen* published in 1906.

The Carmarthenshire poet Lewis Morris was, however, an enthusiastic Welsh advocate of Vaughan's work. Morris's poem 'To an unknown poet', which was addressed to Vaughan, appeared in his very popular collection *Songs of Two Worlds,* which was issued in several editions in the early 1870s. It is difficult to judge how much Morris's passion for Vaughan's poetry stimulated interest amongst his fellow countrymen but in his time, Morris's reputation and popularity was second only to Tennyson. And in April 1891, *The Carmarthen Journal and South Wales Weekly Advertiser* published an article entitled A Welsh Poet of 200 years ago:

7 Grosart, i, pp. xxiii, xxviii.

8 Samuel Lewis, *Topographical Dictionary of Wales* (Llandovery: Lewis, 1833).

9 Nicholas, pp. 82, 95, 102.

10 Robert Williams, *Enwogion Cymru* (Llandovery: William Rees, 1852).

> Our best known Welsh singer of today, Mr. Lewis Morris, has done honour in his pleasant and diversified volume 'Songs of Two Worlds' to our poet of the seventeenth century Henry Vaughan and to his memory, we believe, the book is dedicated. He is a poet more, perhaps, for the studious than the average public, if only for the elevation of thought shown in his verses and the earnestness and sobriety of their range of subject. But there are few who love poetry in any degree who could not find something to suit their taste in his pages, and even those Cambrians who do not (and we believe them the minority) may yet be proud to remember he holds his own among accepted poets and was an undoubted Welshman.[11]

Morris was also one of those contacted by Grosart in his unsuccessful campaign for a memorial window to Vaughan.[12]

Morris also sought other ways to raise the profile and knowledge of Vaughan's works amongst his fellow countrymen. On 27 May 1891, he presided over a meeting of the Cymmrodorion Society in London which was addressed by Francis Palgrave, Professor of Poetry at the University of Oxford, on the subject of *Henry Vaughan of Scethrog: Some Notes on his Life and Characteristics as a Poet of Welsh Descent*. Palgrave, who of course had chosen the poem 'The Retreat' for his Golden Treasury of English Verse published in 1863, described Vaughan as 'the most remarkable among several poets who, though of Welsh descent, and . . . gifted with characteristically Welsh genius, wrote in English'[13] and his daughter later wrote that Vaughan was a 'poet whom my father held in high estimation and whose work he deemed unfamiliar to too many.'[14] Palgrave's talk was repeated two days later in Oxford, 'where it was attended by the dons of Jesus College and almost the entire Welsh colony' and there are a number of references to the subject in newspapers published in Wales in both Welsh and English during the course of 1891.[15]

Again one cannot easily judge how much interest these reports produced in Vaughan's work but it shows that the community of interest was much wider

11 *The Carmarthen Journal and South Wales Weekly Advertiser*, 3rd April, 1891. This and all other newspaper references below were accessed through www. welsh newspapers online.

12 Tennyson, iii, p. 321 fn.

13 Francis Palgrave, 'Henry Vaughan of Scethrog, 1622-95: Some Notes on his life and characteristics as a poet of Welsh descent', in *Cymmrodor* 11(1892), pp. 190-223. Palgrave was himself a Welsh speaker and a regular visitor to Wales.

14 Gwenllian F. Palgrave, *Francis Turner Palgrave. His Journals and Memoirs of his Life*, (London: Longmans and Green, 1899), p. 212.

15 *The Welshman* 6 June 1891. See also *Western Mail*, 29 May 1891; *Y Cymro*, 2 July 1891; *Baner ac Amserau Cymru*, 3 June 1891; *Cardiff Times* 6 June 1891. On 19 February 1895, the *Evening Express* also reported the appointment of Professor John Rhys as Principal of Jesus College, Oxford and recalled that Henry Vaughan was a Jesus alumni.

than just Brecon. Palgrave himself died in 1897, but not before he had contributed to the fund to restore Vaughan's grave, of which more later.

Another advocate of Vaughan's work was the first Lord Aberdare, Henry Austen Bruce, an industrialist and Liberal politician, who served as Home Secretary and Lord President of the Council under Gladstone and was a major influence on Welsh education in the late nineteenth century. Two of Lord Aberdare's letters to members of his family included quotations from the poems of Henry Vaughan[16] and at the 1880 Eisteddfod, which was held in Swansea, Lord Aberdare was reported to have praised Vaughan's poetry.

His comments were hailed by a writer to the *Western Mail* on 30 August 1880, who gave him (or her) self the tag *Iscanus*:

> Allow me . . . to express my gratification at the remarks of Lord Aberdare concerning Henry Vaughan of Newton, Breconshire. The position and character of Lord Aberdare lend weight to his observations and I hope they will lead our young aspirants for eisteddfodic fame to peruse the works of a true and genuine Welsh poet.

The author goes on to state that 'in my feeble way I have endeavoured for the last 15 years to draw the attention of his countrymen' to Vaughan's works' and attributes Vaughan's neglect to sectarian bias which he had himself both foreseen and experienced:

> Henry Vaughan was a churchman and a royalist, so his poetic fire and insight were smothered under the dominant sectarian bias of the last 150 years . . . with the advent of the Church Congress and the British Association to Wales let us hope for the disentombment of some of our buried celebrities, and that they will henceforth occupy their proper place on the pedestals of fame to scatter light and sweetness through our narrow Puritanism, which has hitherto stifled the poetic life and aspiration of the Cymric people, and warped their ideas of true greatness. With the disappearance of sectarian prejudice, Henry Vaughan will shine more and more.[17]

Lord Aberdare was a friend and colleague of Dean Vaughan of Llandaff, who Grosart suggested[18] might have been a descendant of Henry Vaughan, through

16 Henry Austin Bruce, Lord Aberdare, *Letters* (Oxford, 1902), ii, pp. 7, 74-5, 213, 333.

17 A copy of this article is pasted into Joseph's copy of Grosart's edition in the National Library of Wales.

18 Grosart, iv, pp. xl-xlv.

his son William, and at the Eisteddfod in Cardiff in 1883, Dean Vaughan, as President for the day, praised his audience for not allowing:

> an absence of two centuries . . . to wipe out the old memories of the banks of the Usk or to silence in your hearts the saintly melodies of the manor house of Scethrog.[19]

The Dean was later much involved in the campaign to restore the poet's grave at Llansantffraed but the extent to which he had previously promoted the works of his 'ancestor' is not clear. His obituaries make no reference to his family links and many of his papers were destroyed after his death. Grosart, however, wrote in his Preface that Dr. Charles Vaughan of Temple 'one of the most luminous of living sacred authors will gladly own allegiance to the poet of the Usk.'[20]

As a student in 1881, Owen (O.M.) Edwards, later a prominent Welsh educationalist, historian and writer, wrote an article about Henry Vaughan in the University College of Wales magazine, commenting:

> He certainly deserves more attention than he has received and perhaps his beloved Isca will not owe all its celebrity to its beautiful scenery, but will be indebted for some of it to the poet who sang along its banks.[21]

And in August 1885, a question from a visitor to the area prompted J and J Jones of Merthyr Tydfil to find out more about Vaughan and write an article for the *Red Dragon* magazine, which described itself as the National Magazine of Wales.[22]

But if some sought to raise interest in the Breconshire poet, it was insufficient to merit any mention at the reopening of Llansantffraed church in November 1885. Writing in *Old Welsh Chips*, a miscellany of items of local interest published by Edwin Poole of Brecon, in 1888, Gwenllian Morgan declared:

> The coldness and indifference shown towards his works, the ignorance displayed in this, his native county, has often come to us with a sense of surprise and disappointment, his very existence being forgotten or un-

19 See Edwin Poole, *The illustrated Eisteddfod guide to the Borough and County of Brecknock* (Brecon: Poole, 1889), pp. 62-3.

20 Grosart, i, p. xliv. Dean Vaughan's career included the Headmasterhip of Harrow School, Mastership of the Temple in London and finally the Llandaff Deanery.

21 Owen Edwards, 'Henry Vaughan the Silurist' in *University of Wales Magazine*, 2nd December 1881, p. 77.

> known! The most striking instance of this occurred some little time ago at the reopening of the beautiful church of Llansaintffraed, when there was a large representative gathering of the clergy and laity of the neighbourhood, and in the course of several speeches made on that occasion no single speaker mentioned the name of, or in any way referred to, Henry Vaughan . . . Verily a prophet hath no honour in his own country.[23]

And there was similarly no mention of Vaughan in the lengthy report of the event in the *Brecknock County Times*[24], although the church architect, Stephen Williams, provided a sketch of Vaughan's grave and a brief reference to his poetry in his article on the church rebuilding published in *Archaeologia Cambrensis* in 1887.[25]

Gwenllian Morgan had of course been carrying the torch for Vaughan for sometime and contributed several lengthy articles about his life and work to the *Brecon County Times* in 1886/7, which were reprinted the following year in *Old Welsh Chips*.[26] These articles might have been prompted by a letter in September 1886 from *Iscanus* (identified as from Pencelli near Brecon and perhaps also the author of the earlier letter to the *Western Mail*) seeking information about where to find 'an extensive account of the life of the . . . Welsh-English poet and scholar.'[27]

As editor of the *Brecon and Radnor Express*, the local historian and publisher of a number of books about the history of Breconshire, Edwin Poole also did what he could to remind his readers that Vaughan was a notable son of the county. In his *Illustrated History and Biography of Brecknockshire,* published in 1886, Poole lamented that 'the name of Henry Vaughan is hardly known in Wales and his works still less'[28] and in his *Illustrated Guide to the Borough and County of Brecknock,* published in 1889, to coincide with the Eisteddfod at Brecon, he re-emphasised this point, with a chapter on 'Literary Brecknock and Eminent Breconians':

22 J. and J. Jones, 'Henry Vaughan, The Silurist', in *Red Dragon,* 8 (1885), 165-74.

23 Gwenllian Morgan, *Old Welsh Chips,* 1888, pp. 7-8.

24 The article perhaps understandably focused on the benefaction of the Gwynne Holford family. The *Brecknock County Times* is not currently available on www.welsh newspapers online, but is accessible on microfilm at Brecon Library.

25 Stephen W. Williams, 'Llansaintffraed, Llanhamlach and Llanfigan churches', *Archaeologia Cambrensis 5th series* 4 (1887), 202-13.

26 Morgan, "Henry Vaughan, Silurist', in *Old Welsh Chips* (1888), pp. 7-13, 40-47, 319-25, 346-50.

27 *Western Mail,* 10th August 1883. See also Edwin Poole, *The Illustrated History and Biography of Brecknockshire* (Brecknock, 1886), pp. 137-8.

28 Poole, pp. 324-6.

> The county of Brecknock and the shire town especially has not only a brilliant historical past, but our home literary annals are neither few nor unimportant. Many literary 'men and women of note' have been born or bred, or otherwise intimately connected with Breconshire . . .
>
> Among poets we have the name of the gifted Henry Vaughan, 'Silurist' a second George Herbert, whose muse, like that of Herbert's sang of the deeper things affecting the eternal destiny of man. Henry Vaughan sleeps the sleep of the just in Llansaintfraed churchyard, a few miles out of Brecon, and, strange to say, very few people in the county know even his name, leave alone the deep merits of his sacred poetry.

Poole reminded his Eisteddfodic readers of the tributes paid to Vaughan by Lord Aberdare and Dean Vaughan at previous Eisteddfods and concluded:

> Not till then, we repeat, did the general body of Welshmen appear to know that Wales in general, and Breconshire in particular, is indebted for the living in Scethrog manor house of a poet of the first order; English literateurs have done greater justice to Silurist's work.[29]

The influence of the Eisteddfod tributes is again difficult to gauge but ripples do seem to have spread well beyond Brecon and one can find references to Vaughan's life and work in unexpected places. Thus on 26 February 1886, the Welsh weekly language newspaper *Y Dydd* published an article about Vaughan entitled *Bardd rhagorol a Chymro glan gloyw* declaring that it was to the everlasting credit of Wales that it was the country of birth and burial place of Henry Vaughan the Silurist.

The article seems to have been stimulated by a piece in *The Presbyterian Review* in 1880 by an American Presbyterian Minister from Philadelphia, Dr. Samuel Duffield. He had written that 'it would be difficult to find a true and lofty singer who has been so seriously underrated as Vaughan' and praised two gentleman whose work had rescued Vaughan 'from oblivion'- Rev. Francis Lyte, who of course edited Vaughan's work in 1847, and George Macdonald.[30]

Duffield was probably thinking of Macdonald's *England's Antiphon*, his study of English religious poetry published in 1868, which included a chapter on Vaughan, entitled 'A Mount of Vision'. He was, however, also a prolific novelist

29 Edwin Poole, *The Illustrated Eisteddfod Guide to the Borough and County of Brecknock* (Brecknock: Poole, 1889), pp. 62-3.

30 Samuel Duffield, 'Henry Vaughan, the Poet of Light', *Presbyterian Review* 1 (1880), pp. 291-303.

and Henry Vaughan features in several of his fictional works, with quotations from his poetry in, for example, the novel *David Elginbrod*, published in 1863. Indeed in one novel, *St George and St Michael*, published in 1875, Vaughan appears in person visiting his cousin the heroine Dorothy Vaughan, at Raglan Castle, against the background of the Civil War. The novel also features Vaughan's former tutor, Matthew Herbert, visiting the castle from his rectory in Llangattock.[31]

Vaughan was also the subject of a letter in January 1886 to the journal *Y Geninen*, a quarterly journal in Welsh, which aimed to provide a forum for the discussion of literary, political, social and religious issues. The author, Ioan Ddu, who seems to have been a regular correspondent on literary matters, lamented the neglect of Vaughan's work in favour of lesser poets who wrote in Welsh and provided a translation of one poem into Welsh to prove his point.[32] Indeed a Vaughan poem was even chosen for the English to Welsh translation competition at the Eisteddfod in 1893.[33]

Nevertheless, when she visited Llansantffraed in the summer of 1895, Louise Guiney found his grave much neglected.[34] Her campaign started in *The Athenaeum* was, however, soon taken on locally by Gwenllian Morgan, and seems to have stimulated much interest with a variety of reports in Welsh newspapers. In October 1895, the *South Wales Daily News* referred to an American Lady's timely appeal and accepted that 'Wales is often justly accused of continuing to neglect the unhonoured ashes of her greatest sons.'[35] And Gwenllian Morgan's papers in the National Library of Wales[36] include a letter to the editor of the Daily Graphic in November 1895 from Arlunydd Penygarn, with an accompanying sketch, done on his own visit to the grave, which continued the ashes theme:

> Attention has been called recently to the neglected state of the grave of Henry Vaughan, the "Silurist". I beg to send you a sketch of its present condition. If the coal-hut and ash-box were removed, the grave itself would not be unworthy of a poet, for an ancient yew bends over it, and the slab is furred over by delicate green lichen, which turns to gold in the

31 George Macdonald, *Saint George and Saint Michael* (1876), mpp. 1-3, 24, 30, 53-5, 237-40.

32 *Y Geninen,* Ionawr 1 (1886), 4 (1), p. 69.

33 *Y Llan* 15 August 1893.

34 See Elizabeth Siberry and Robert Wilcher, eds., *Henry Vaughan and the Usk Valley* (Little Logaston: Logaston, 2016) and Jonathan Naumann, 'Louise Imogen Guiney and Henry Vaughan', *Brycheiniog* 48 (2017), pp. 98-112.

35 *South Wales Daily News* 16 October 1895.

36 NLW GEFM box 1 file 5 envelope 16.

> occasional gleams of sunshine. In the silence of the place the ripple of the author's beloved Usk can be heard. Oddly enough, excepting the grave, the churchyard is in "apple-pie" order, the conifers with which it is planted having even little labels of iron before them bearing their botanical names and habitat. But the slab is largely covered with cinders, which I pushed back to sketch the inscription. No doubt the rubric does direct "ashes to ashes" but the good folk of Llansantffraed have complied with a ridiculous generosity.[37]

The correspondent, Arlunydd Penygarn, was in fact Thomas Henry Thomas, an artist who became a special correspondent for *The Graphic* and *Daily Graphic* newspapers and took a close interest in Welsh matters. No other letters by Thomas relating to Vaughan seem to have survived but it is another indication of the ripple effect from Guiney's visit. [38]

Grosart also read of the appeal and wrote to *The Athenaeum* in November 1895 expressing his support and recalling his previous attempts to provide a suitable memorial to Vaughan:

> When I completed my new edition . . . I wrote a number of letters to likely persons suggesting a modest monument, either at Llansantffraed or in Jesus College, Oxford. Save that my letters brought me sympathetic answers from Lord Tennyson, Lord Chief Justice Coleridge, Robert Browning, and two or three others, the outcome was so meager that I had reluctantly to abandon my project. Specifically, the rector of Vaughan's church and custodian of his dust showed astonishing ignorance and unconcern, if I might not say hostility. Miss Guiney tells us that he now 'seems to have some knowledge of him'. I am glad to hear of it. Successive splashes of cold water were all I had from Wales and Welshmen.[39]

The list of subscribers to the Memorial Fund, now in the National Library amongst the Gwenllian Morgan papers, provides some further insight into those whose interest in Vaughan had been either awakened or reawakened by the appeal. Louise Guiney and her travelling companion Alice Brown were obvious contributors, along with some other American admirers. Isabel Southall from Edgbaston, who composed a poem about Vaughan's grave, and Vaughan's

37 *The Daily Graphic*, 8 November 1895.

38 Christabel Hutchings, ed. *The Correspondence of Thomas Henry Thomas 'Arlunydd Penygarn'*, (Newport: South Wales Record Society, 2012).

39 *The Athenaeum*, 30 November, 1895, p. 756.

editors, Grosart and John Tutin also contributed, as did a number of members of the Vaughan family; Canon Rawnsley from Cumbria one of the founders of the National Trust and himself a poet, and some local notables from Brecon, including Mrs. Cobb, whose late husband, Joseph Cobb was a leading Welsh antiquarian and had played a key role in the restoration of the Priory Church in Brecon.

Gwenllian Morgan apart, however, the prime mover seems to have been Dean Vaughan, although persistent ill-health prevented him from actually visiting Llansantffraed. A T. C. Thomas of Llandaff wrote to the *Weekly Mail* in May 1897 (after the ceremony unveiling the plaque to Vaughan at Llansantffraed church), recording his visit to the grave with the sentiment 'better late than never'. His local links then prompted him to remind the editor that:

> the Silurist was an ancestor of our Venerable Dean Vaughan, who in some respects resembles, but in many more transcends, the illustrious Silurist.[40]

Dean Vaughan's achievements seem in practice to have been more related to the work of church and state than literature[41] and it is not clear that he was in fact descended from the poet. He was, however, a significant contributor to the restoration fund and in the words of Gwenllian Morgan, took 'the deepest interest in the project'. He was also the author of the inscription on the memorial tablet now on the south wall of the church.

There are also some hints of tensions between the Dean and local Vaughan enthusiasts. An annotation in Gwenllian Morgan's copy of the Edmund Chambers' edition highlights the last 5 lines of the poem *The Book* and comments (with her own underlining) 'a fitting epitaph for his tablet <u>not</u> what was chosen.[42] And there was some lively correspondence about the fund and restoration in the *Brecon and Radnor Express.* [43]

A correspondent using the tag an *Intending Subscriber* complained first that the work to restore the grave was being carried out by a firm in Llandaff:

> Is Mr. Clarke[44] a Breconshire man? And if not, may I ask if it would not be more fitting that a Breconshire man should restore a Breconshire poet's

40 *Weekly Mail*, 22 May 1897.

41 See Trevor Park, *'Nolo Epsicolari' A Life of C J Vaughan* (St. Bees: St Bega Publications) 2013.

42 Edmund Chambers, ed. *Poems of Henry Vaughan Silurist* (London: Routledge, 1925), ii p. 286. The quotation is from the copy in the author's possession.

43 The press cutting, like a number collected by Gwenllian Morgan, is undated.

44 The work was carried out by the Llandaff based firm W. Clarke which is still in business, but unfortunately no records have survived of the Llansantffraed project.

> tomb, especially as there are many competent to do so? It would, in my opinion, have been a much better plan, and one that would have commended itself to all those interested in Henry Vaughan's works (and certainly to Breconshire readers) that a county committee were appointed to take the matter in hand, and that a tradesman from one of the neighbouring towns should carry out the work.

The same correspondent also complained about the use of public subscriptions to remove the ashpit and for a memorial in the church. He questioned why, if he could prove descent from the poet, Dean Vaughan had allowed the grave to 'get into and to remain in, the condition it now is' and argued that if a tablet was required, then Thomas Vaughan would be a more appropriate subject:

> I have already heard severe condemnation of the proposal to remove the ashpit with public subscriptions and I shall be greatly surprised if such disapproval does not find loud expression . . . Most subscribers, I feel sure would (also) say that their duty to the memory of Henry Vaughan had ended with a decent restoration of his tomb, and that it would not extend to another within the church.

We only have Gwenllian Morgan's copies of the local press cuttings, so cannot tell how widespread such views may have been. In any event, the campaign to restore the grave seems to have rekindled some Welsh interest in Vaughan's work and at the Cardiff meeting of the Cymmrodorion in December 1897, the Rev. Howell Elvet 'Elfed' Lewis a Congregational minister who had begun his career at Buckley, not far from Gladstone's home at Hawarden, Flintshire and knew Palgrave, delivered a lecture on Henry Vaughan. Lewis noted a resemblance between Vaughan's work and that of Wordsworth and two other wordsmiths of Wales-Islwyn and the great hymnwriter Williams Pantycelyn. Again a link was drawn with Dean Vaughan, whose funeral had been held in Llandaff cathedral in October that year:

> While they in Cardiff were contemplating the perpetuation of the memory of the late Dean of Llandaff, the Vaughan of the century, he was glad to remind them of another celebrated Vaughan of two centuries ago.[45]

One much earlier Breconshire writer who had referred to Vaughan was of course Theophilus Jones, whose *History of Brecknockshire* was published in

45 *Weekly Mail* 18 December 1897. See also Prys Morgan, 'The Golden Treasurer: F.T. Palgrave and the Cymmrodorion', in *Cymmrodorion*, n.s. 17 (2011), pp. 80-86.

1805. His account was rather confused and a reprint in 1898 provided an opportunity to provide some context. The *Western Mail* of 18 October 1898 commented that Jones's 'conduct towards Henry Vaughan, though not praise-worthy, is at least defensible' and quoted Gwenllian Morgan's views on this subject at some length. She had argued that Jones would have had little access to editions of Vaughan's work for:

> it is doubtful whether anyone then living appreciated the Silurist except Wordsworth, who had a marked copy of *Silex scintillans* in his cottage at Grasmere.

Morgan returned to this subject in her contribution to the life of Theophilus Jones published in 1905 and provides some further local insight into what was known about Thomas and Henry Vaughan in their local area at the beginning of the nineteenth century when Jones was writing his history:

> He faithfully wrote down all that he knew and heard of them, and when we remember that Denys/Denise Jones, Henry Vaughan's grand-daughter,[46] was living in Brecon at the same time as Theophilus Jones's parents, it is probable that he reflected the true impression of contemporary public opinion respecting the Vaughans. Mr. Jones's assertion, that he had not been able to trace any of their descendants, and that the line had become extinct, has not yet been refuted, though of recent years the closest search has been made on the subject. To blame him for not appreciating the Silurist's poems, which he had not read, is hardly criticism.[47]

As we have seen, however, others claimed family links with Henry Vaughan perhaps more based on a shared surname than detailed genealogical research.

The 1851 Catalogue of books in the Brecon Literary, Scientific and Mechanics Institution did not include any of Vaughan's works and the limited availability of modern editions of Vaughan's works until the latter part of the nineteenth century may be a practical explanation for limited local knowledge and interest. But, as the turn of the century approached, Wales (both English and Welsh speaking and writing) seems to have known and celebrated more of the life

46 Francis Hutchinson, *Henry Vaughan. A Life and Interpretation* (Oxford: Clarendon, 1947), p. 251 notes that she was the latest descendant of the poet who could be traced.

47 Edwin Davies, *Theophilus Jones, F.S.A. Historian: His Life, Letters and Literary Remains* (Brecon: Davies and Co. 1906) p. 19.

and work of Henry Vaughan and even in the less informed earlier years, he found some enthusiastic readers, not only in Brecon, but elsewhere in his home country.[48]

In 1909, the recently founded National Library of Wales at Aberystwyth held its first open and free exhibition of rare books and manuscripts and newspapers reported that the items on display included a first edition of *Olor Iscanus* with its fine title page and that the Sir John Williams collection (which formed the foundation of the library) included an 'extensive series of the works of Henry Vaughan' and his brother Thomas.[49] In fact Sir John Williams, a Welsh born London physician who attended Queen Victoria, but is now known more for his benefaction to the Library, seems to have made a particular point of collecting the works of Henry and Thomas Vaughan, with two copies of *Olor Iscanus*; two of *Silex scintillans* (one with the bookplate of the poet William Cowper) and two again of *Flores solitudinis* now in the collection at Aberystwyth.[50] Sir John began his serious collecting in the 1870s and research into the chronology and provenance of his and other collections in Wales might shed further light on interest in Henry Vaughan during the nineteenth century. For example, the Library also has a 1651 edition of Olor Iscanus with a bookplate of a W. A. Vaughan, which was donated by another key figure in its early history, the Welsh lawyer, John Humphreys Davies and an edition of Grosart which belonged to Lord Coleridge, who was consulted about a memorial to Henry Vaughan.[51]

William Gladstone's library at Hawarden, Flintshire also included several editions of Vaughan's works, with minor annotations. His diaries also record him reading Vaughan's works in February 1863; November 1872; June 1874 and November 1886.[52]

In any event, by the early 1900s, it is much easier to find references to Henry Vaughan in guides to Brecknockshire[53] and as today, walkers and readers made

48 Other members of the Vaughan family also seem to have highlighted their connection with the poet. In the *Weekly Mail* of 26 May 1906, it was noted that the recently deceased Sir James Vaughan, a London magistrate born in Cardiff, was 'descended from Henry Vaughan of Brecon, the celebrated poet.'

49 *Cardiff Times* 23 January 1909 and *Aberystwyth Observer* 22 July 1909.

50 Noel Jerman, The 'Sir John Williams Collection', *National Library of Wales Journal 1(4)* 1940, p. 205.

51 I am grateful to Timothy Cutts, Rare Books Librarian at the National Library, for this information about the Vaughan editions at Aberystwyth.

52 www.gladstoneslibrary.org and Henry Matthew, ed. *The Gladstone Diaires* (Oxford: University Press, 1994).

53 See for example Arthur Bradley, *Highways and Byways of Wales* (London: Macmillan, 1903), pp. 394-6 and *In the March and Borderland of Wales* (London: Constable, 1906), p. 114.

their pilgrimages to Vaughan's grave at Llansantffraed.[54] Gwenllian Morgan also continued to collect tributes to Vaughan and exchanged letters with other poets and literary commentators up until her death in 1939. Her papers in Aberystwyth include a number of poems (of variable quality) inspired by visits to Vaughan's grave, including one dated 1911 by the Carmarthenshire post John Jenkins, who took the bardic name Gwili. He wrote in the *Brecon and Radnor Express* in November 1911 of his visit to the grave where he laid a wreath:

So rest, thou jewel of the just
While pilgrims seek thy flowering dust
Thou canst not spurn the fading wretha
I place upon thy beauteous death
Until the Dawn.[55]

The way in which Henry Vaughan was remembered and celebrated in Wales in the nineteenth century therefore seems to be rather more varied than might first appear.

54 *The Aberdare Leader* 17 September 1910. The group in question was the NUT Rambling Club.

55 Exchange of letters with Huw Menai, Huw Owen Williams, a Caernarvonshure poet, Caernarvonshire Western Mail.

Pathway
by Colin See-Paynton

PETER LIMBRICK

Wavicle

Science tells us the answers we get
are limited by the cleverness of
the questions we ask.

Thus, our crude questions about light
brought contradictory answers
involving waves or particles.

So, it is no more, 'Do you love me?'
but, 'When is our difference?'
and, 'What is the time between us?'

ROSE FLINT

September Tenancies at Witham

Some leaves are lucent as their young selves in May
yellow as harvest butter, last fires burning
through threads of the matrix, sky bird-egg blue.
Last week, my son saw an otter here in the river
at our front door. It entered the swimming hole,
climbed the old mill steps, going upstream
under the road to where the bridge
makes a perfect circle, framing a place of light
that shines green-gold as the promised land.
I think my son must be loved by otters
to be allowed to witness their secret lives.

High on the swoop of the shed roof
Himalayan Balsam – so many peachy baby mouths
in felicity – sways with a weight of sipping insects.
I should cut it soon, cull it for its innocent power
of disruption, but I remember the tiny white
murmuring bees that drowsed on its pollen
in a Lancashire valley of massed beeches
and bandstands. As if white bees came from far
snows, cosseted emissaries snug in a cell of ice
gliding down on a wing of cirrostratus.

We are unsettled, unrooted, and will move on,
my son soon as the third brood of swallows.
Each season has brought its own nomads: last winter
swans and great egrets, rumours of cranes,
three greylag geese on the day my grandson chose
to be born. July saw the grace of a lammergeyer
astray from south floating over. This is how it goes
since the ice thinned, and birch and aspen came in
from the arctic taiga: land and living changing colours
in kaleidoscopes of gains and losses.

I don't know who will come to make this their home
in the shifting sequences of tenancies and weather;
moving on is hard, tears at the heart, folds danger
into earth, air, water. The path out to Witham
winds up high under vines and bamboo, but here
after hard rain the river rises fast towards flood,
meringues of foam caught twisting in dry angelica.
I watch the changing light flickering like hope
on that other route out of here, the one the otters take:
trackless through drowning black deep, up
against the flow of swollen water that falls in thunder,
but still on, to slip through the lit curve into a spaciousness
that seems bright and tender as some future of love.

Lake Lilies

How hard the lilies work
bringing up their weight of beauty

their leaves falter and overturn
float brown-roan, chestnut-pink

cockled up until
a fuzz of white

breathes buds and stars themselves
on browngreen water

Rising now into summer
leaving the world under

to their old selves, stems are steel
all whipcord and curve

power enough to haul
whole new landscapes into life.

EVE JACKSON

Swan Feathers

In the moments of ruffle and rearranging their cloud
of plumage, when braking, or at that point they walk
on water, swans perfect the art of being angels. They trample

their own reflections to lift themselves to something beyond
our reach. An undulation of wings embraces layers of space
between water and sky; an immaculate harvest of light: particles

of brightness cradled between ripples on river or lake, ruches
of rosettes that moorhens and ducks donate. The glint and sparkle
that trickles from an oar when it dips and pours what it finds beneath.

Pulling a power of whiteness with them, feathers thicken
to heavy snow, packed ice, or three fresh coats of chalk matt white.
A dazzle of distant window, inside, a cotton sheet tethers

a stiff shift of bones. A skull turns; eyes watch a lone feather float down
to rock on the sill. This as the whump, whump of a flat tyre uphill,
or slow-throat swallows that swamp the inner ear

as swans pass low overhead, taking themselves elsewhere. And,
for a brief moment, the room invites their shadows in, as if
crossing itself again and again.

SEÁN STREET

The Stone Bird

Soon it is Spring
and standing stones
are on the march
chasing the gaze
of the season.

I heard someone
carving birdsong
heard a singing,
old stone on stone.

Morning cutting
down into rock
always finds voice.

CAROLINE NATZLER

Pre-history

Stick warriors bristle
alongside lances and tilting swords
incised into cracked stone

chariots seen from the sky
horses' legs, insect thin, splayed out
as if a weight had fallen on them.

Some figures bear small discs on handles
mirrors, the label says.
Why would warriors need mirrors?

Maybe - the thought pricks -
they're for scrying what is to come

for we walk backwards
into the future, unseeing.

Some ancient cultures such as the Greeks and peoples of the near East conceived of us as going backwards into the future, since it cannot be seen.

HELEN MOORE

Seed Yoga Sutra

The firm flesh of you, pea-sized vegetable body
crouched in sodden crumbs,

a dun oilskin pulled tight around your neck,
like a farmer trudging through sleet.

Inside your raw, sour orb (this power-house
of singular intention), my mind curls,

sensing the pulse of energy as tissues swell
to burst every seam of your coat.

Soon your radicle will descend – pointy teenage
tip, a pale straw to suck the chill soup,

and sprouting ticklish hairs, twitching
as invertebrates attend to soil engineering.

No particle of your being questions
your purpose, which confirms every cell;

nor do you fear injury, potential destruction
(the hoe's cold-shoulder, frost's iron grasp).

Steadfast is the mode of your two-fold
extension – seed yoga sutra,

an impeccable asana, rootlet below
as your plumule burrows up to sunlight.

There, unfurling twin cotyledons,
you're seedling with janus heads,

one to look forward, one back – but no fixation
on time to come or gone. *Present moment,*

perfect moment, your mantra – yet you lean to stimuli
that favour self-expression. As Spring stirs,

I too become surrendered in this dance,
where purpose meets the spiral waves of chance.

MICHAEL HENRY

Petrichor

Cities have an ancestral smell,
as if there were beautiful brioches
of horse manure steaming on the streets.
And deep down underneath a hint
    of ammonia.

Towns should have olfactory crests.
Skegness, where I couldn't stand the smell
of dead whale on the Lincolnshire beach,
tons of blubber rotting and reeking
    of mildew and middens.

And there's the dank anthracite dust smell
of the industrial heartlands where names
have a strong masculine breath
and the sun is sometimes embarrassed
    to shine.

I recall the dominant satirical smells –
sauerkraut, the second German word
I learned; onions and garlic dressed
in blue berets; the listed smell
    of Paris *pissoirs*.

Recreational smells in campers, narrowboats:
paraffin fluttering an unsteady blue flame;
a charred bottom-of-the-pan smell;
sweaters with spray-on fresh air
    or wood-smoke.

And the *jolie laide* odours
of leaf-mould and the whiff
of forest-fear that comes
with owl-song and predators
    in the night.

And everywhere, petrichor,
the smell of dry earth after a shower,
released over the fields like a prayer.
In our anosmic society we are missing
so much and so much.

LESLEY SAUNDERS

Showing, Not Telling

'...some words and phrases, such as "me" or "here", cannot be fully understood without additional contextual information.'

Out there on Wide-Awake Hill the white-faced owl
is asking to be lip-read as psyche, as cipher or semaphore,
a child's name in the ark of a mother's mouth.

Out there in the freezing fog every edge is blunted,
every shape is a grey ghost cast by the meagre search-beam
of the hunter's mind on the haunted light.

In here where the blizzard is thickest, the house wears
a caul of frost-fur and all the spent chandeliers are ice-harps,
we play our own version of lost in the dark.

But someplace where the storm has washed us, a radio
fills the sky with verilys and ding-dongs: the self's high holydays
are numberless. I knew you were you all along.

CHRIS PREDDLE

Perspective

The maker of madonnas Raphael
composed her, in her own high renaissance
seated in a loggia, or file
of columns diminishing like men to a fair horizon.

She is startled by the impertinent
Annunciation of an inmate soul not hers. Horizontals
extend to a vanishing point
from the chequerwork floor of faience tiles.

He made her from no Venus or ragazza
of his own, but a meagre cat of the Vatican gardens
on a counter-diagonal bench narrowed

in perspective to an extenuation. Those now at large
and living, go by her gradual loggia
thinning as they go like the common road.

Roland and Aude

This hill, she thought, or cone
from which all curving forms and mine are taken,
is high land en France dulce
held by Franks for Christ as far as the dulse
of the sea. Roland never lay in my arms,
Roland-in-arms. We were set for sorrow.
Spain is a silk brocade for pagan emirs
to lie on. Christendom will end, laid down in cere.

All the west was our sacred
human order, its long lines secured
to a point, a pontifex in Aix. A mason
made this terrace wall of stones Mycenaean
tied in like holy kingdoms. There's beauty in order.
Violets blue, plant us in fives,
sweet violets, violets blue. But men would undo
sweet Roland, for all I gave him violet favours.

Each hillock and Hissarlik
they fight for (gallopy, gallop) has a carousel Achilles
go round go round with a horse-drawn body.
Let us, of Carolus all, his scattered bodies,
cohere, one body. O my Roland, we
were lovers made by the peace at Vienne
an emperor made. It was in May. This hill is where
imperial dead like standing forms convene.

SARAH LINDON

Icework

Ice has started ceding the lake
and tufted ducks eye all.
The sky contracts,
its blue polish paled
by cold. And somewhere
you watch the same
eggshell of subzero air
and ice on a darkening
pond. As the sun subsides
you send me an image
of its low gold
overflow in branches,
a dry stone wall, indifference
of a sheep and a pony
in its blanket, fields
that rise and fold over hills,
meeting each other,
meeting the hedgerows.

A father and child throw
pieces of ice onto the lake's
frozen surface, which skitter
and shatter and send rods
of vibration through
the delicate expanse,
like compacted echoes,
shooting compressions,
or like stinging connections
in the crackles and twangs
of the air around pylons.
When night comes
the lake will grip those fragments
till they bond.

There is Nothing Automatic

in the joy I take from the startled herons
clambering off the riverbed
and into air, though I regret
their punch-drunk retreat.

At what speed do their hearts beat?
I have set them off by running
beside the water and now they wade
above the treetops as if migrating.

Herons fly with giant puppetry -
unhurryable as hope.
They stop in grey places.
When they watch
they are sculpture.

Perched on tree or roof
they make daylight venerable
the horizon distant
and living an incidental conundrum
with which my jogging feet
are welcome to busy themselves.

The Sonnet Made New in George Herbert's 'The Temple'

SEAN H. MCDOWELL

In the introduction to her monumental edition of *The English Poems of George Herbert*, Helen Wilcox remarks that '*The Temple* owes a great deal to the sonnet sequences of worldly love that were all the rage at the time of Herbert's youth'.[1] Herbert's interest in the sonnet form likely derived from his participation in the Herbert-Sidney family dialogue. He was an insider in some of the most significant English literary conversations about the lyric during the turn of the seventeenth century.[2] In the words of Debra Rienstra, 'Coterie exchange of verse was part of young George's family culture, a family that included Mary Sidney Herbert, her son William Herbert, George's brother Edward, friends John Donne and Benjamin Rudyerd, and of course, always, the ghost of Sir Philip Sidney'[3]. Herbert's earliest known poetic compositions, the two poems he sent to his mother Magdalene Herbert Danvers in 1610, were both sonnets, written soon after and perhaps in response to the publication of Shakespeare's *Sonnets* in 1609. Poems throughout 'The Church', the central section of lyrics in *The Temple*, including some of Herbert's most well-known lyrics–'Jordan (II)', for example–pointedly reference some of the sonnets in Sidney's *Astrophil and Stella*. Meanwhile, the sonnet form engaged Herbert's interest throughout his poetic career.[4] From the beginning to the end of his poetic life, extant sonnets, as examples to resist ('Who says that fictions onely

1 Helen Wilcox, ed., *The English Poems of George Herbert* (Cambridge: Cambridge University Press, 2007), xxiii. Unless otherwise specified, all quotations of Herbert's poetry come from this edition, hereafter referred to as '*Poems*'.

2 For more on this dialogue, see especially Christina Malcolmson, *George Herbert: A Literary Life* (New York: Palgrave Macmillan, 2004), and Jeffrey Powers-Beck, *Writing the Flesh: The Herbert Family Dialogue* (Pittsburgh: Duquesne University Press, 1998).

3 '"Let Wits Contest": George Herbert and the English Sonnet Sequence', *George Herbert Journal* 35.1 & 2 (Fall 2011/Spring 2012): 23.

4 Herbert wrote a total seventeen sonnets. In addition to his two youthful sonnets, Herbert wrote fifteen additional sonnets for *The Temple*. Nine of these ('The Passion' [i.e., 'Redemption'], 'The Sinner', 'H. Baptisme [I]', 'Love [I] and [II]', 'Prayer [I]', 'The H. Scriptures [I] and [II]', and 'Christmas-day' [i.e., the first part of 'Christmas') appear in the Williams manuscript, that gathering of seventy-eight poems Herbert had professionally copied as an intermediate step in his

and false hair/Become a verse?'), and the sonnet form, as a means of giving voice to emotional urgencies ('. . . though my hard heart scarce can grone, /Remember that thou once did write on stone'), informed that fervor of inspiration that drove Herbert to bring 'every dimension of poetry . . . into the service of God.'[5] It was as if a fundamental part of Herbert's desire to re-purpose the eloquent poetry of his time for divine service necessitated direct engagement with the sonnet itself for a variety of expressive purposes.

When he came to write his own sonnets, however, the one purpose Herbert scrupulously avoided was the articulation of amorous desire. While fascinated by some structural possibilities of the form, both as a stand-alone poem and as part of a larger whole, as in the case of 'Christmas', he nonetheless resisted its implicit associations with a personalized amorousness, especially as depicted by the English Petrarchan sonneteers of the late sixteenth century. The inventive poetic experimenter, the maker of what Mary Ellen Rickey called the 'utmost art', the poet's poet whose work Seamus Heaney memorably foregrounded in 1989 as a primary example of a 'fully realized poetry that thrives beyond the exigencies of the merely political',[6] Herbert *chose* to exclude the one psychological condition most commonly linked by his contemporaries to his chosen form. Instead, he denuded the sonnet of its conventional trappings, stripped the form of its Petrarchan garb, and thereby opened it to service of other non-amorous devotional and expressive purposes.

As a consequence of this repurposing of the sonnet, readers who encounter Herbert's mature sonnets for the first time may not be aware that the poems *are* sonnets upon a first reading. As John H. Ottenhoff notes, Herbert's sonnets 'depart from the expected sonnet form in diverse and complex ways', while Virginia R. Mollenkott describes these poems as notable 'especially in their experimental freedom'.[7] Within *The Temple*, Herbert's sonnets tend to be

ongoing composition process. He must have written these before or during 1623. John Drury gives the 1623 dating based on the three Latin poems addressed to Urban VIII, who became pope in 1623 (*Music at Midnight: The Life & Poetry of George Herbert* [Chicago: Chicago University Press, 2014], 139). Amy Charles, in *The Williams Manuscript of George Herbert's Poems* (Delmar, New York: Scholars' Facsimiles & Reprints, 1977, xx-xxi), speculates Herbert could have been composed during one or both of Herbert's "free" or unemployed periods in 1613-1614 or in 1616-1617. Herbert added six more sonnets ('Sinne [I]', 'Avarice', 'The Holdfast', 'Joseph's coat', 'The Sonne', and 'The Answer') later as *The Temple* reached its final form.

5 *Poems*, xxiii.

6 Heaney, *The Redress of Poetry* (New York: Farrar, Strauss, and Giroux, 1995), 10.

7 See Ottenhoff, 'Herbert's Sonnets', *George Herbert Journal* 2.2 (1979): 1-14; and Mollenkott, 'Experimental Freedom in Herbert's Sonnets', *Christian Scholar's Review* 1 (1971): 109-116. Mollenkott credits Herbert with a formal innovation she considers a 'minor but distinctive contribution to the English sonnet tradition: a third quatrain with an enveloped rather than an alternating rhyme scheme' (110). For an additional analysis of Herbert's experimentation with the form, this time in comparison with Donne's use of 'binding' images of contraries, see also Jerome Mazzaro, 'Donne and Herbert: Striking Through the Mask: Herbert and Donne at Sonnets' in *Like Season'd Timber: New Essays on George Herbert*, ed. Edmund Miller (New York: Peter Lang, 1997), 241-54.

tucked individually within groupings of poems that vary considerably in length, stanza, and line construction. 'The Sinner', for example, the first sonnet to appear in 'The Church', follows after the hieroglyph 'The Altar', the sixty-three stanzas of 'The Sacrifice', 'The Thanksgiving' (fifty lines), 'The Reprisal' (sixteen lines), and 'The Agonie' (eighteen lines). 'Good Friday', a 32-line poem containing two sections that employ different stanza forms, immediately follows 'The Sinner'. Then comes 'Redemption', the second sonnet in the collection. There follow three poems with radically different stanza patterns, before we encounter 'H. Baptisme (I)', which is a sonnet, and 'H. Baptisme (II)', which is not. None of these first three sonnets, nor the twelve that appear later, advertise themselves as sonnets the way Shakespeare's do. No titles announce their form; no numbers locate them within a sequence as is the case of the secular *Astrophil and Stella* (itself a collection of multiple forms) or the religious sonnets of Henry Lok or Barnabe Barnes. The last feature points to a substantial difference between Herbert and most other sonneteers of his time: with the possible exception of his two youthful 'New Year Sonnets', that earnest two-part renunciation of poetic praise of feminine beauty, and of 'Love (I) and (II)' and 'The H. Scriptures (I) and (II)', which are presented as two-part poems, Herbert did not write his sonnets as part of sonnet sequences the way most of his predecessors and contemporaries did. Instead, his sonnets, like all the other lyrics in 'The Church', are arranged in non-genre-specific thematic and developmental groupings that give no pride of place to any particular form.

That Herbert's sonnets hide (for lack of a better term) among other poems is one reason why their sonnet-ness is often not immediately apparent. Yet the more striking reason is the assiduousness of Herbert's erasure of most of the conventional content, traditional associations, and widely shared concerns that connected many Elizabethan and Stuart sonnets with Petarchism, however tenuously at times. Herbert claims the form for the exploration of non-amorous emotions and considerations. The sonnet was supposed to be affectively charged. George Puttenham, in one of the few references to it in *The Arte of English Poesy* (1598), associates the sonnet with the conveyance of heightened emotions, especially those of lovers:

> And because love is of all other human affections the most puissant and passionate, and most general to all sorts and ages of men and women, so as whether it be of young or old, or wise or holy, or high estate or low, none ever could truly brag of any exemption in that case, it requireth a form of poesy variable, inconstant, affected, curious, and most witty of any others, whereof the joys were to be uttered in one sort, the sorrows in another, and by the many forms of poesy, the many moods and pangs of lovers throughly to be discovered; the poor souls sometimes praying,

> beseeching; sometime honoring, advancing, praising; another while railing, reviling, and cursing; then sorrowing, weeping, lamenting; in the end laughing, rejoicing, and solacing the beloved again, with a thousand delicate devices, odes, songs, elegies, ballads, sonnets, and other ditties, moving one way and another to great compassion.[8]

Puttenham's description, published two years before the posthumous printing of Sidney's *Astrophil and Stella* in 1591, nicely foreshadows the affective disorders and vicissitudes Elizabethan and Stuart sonnets regularly dramatized throughout the period of the sonnet's greatest popularity in England. The mercurial Herbert, who, according to his brother Edward, battled choler for much of his life, certainly conveys the waxing and waning of strong passions in many lyrics throughout *The Temple*. Strangely, though, he tends to avoid doing so in his sonnets. Either he turns down the emotional heat in these poems or he takes care to avoid any associations with amorous longing. As a result, he develops a different ethos than one typically finds in the early seventeenth-century sonnet, either secular or religious, as the form encompasses a greater range of subjects and situations than in the work of previous English religious sonneteers. By redefining the role of the sonnet in poetic sequence and by denuding the sonnet of its traditional non-formal trappings, Herbert discovers a new originality of invention and expression. He makes the sonnet new.

'Reversed Thunder'

Herbert was not the first to denude the sonnet of amorous or courtly trappings, of course. In the sixteenth century, previous English poets sought to claim the sonnet for religion through this same means. Indeed, Anne Lok adopted it in her *A Meditation of a Penitent Sinner: Written in Maner of a Paraphrase upon the* 51. Pslame of Dauid (1560), the first sonnet sequence in English. Yet Herbert was one of the first to do so while still mindful of the Sidnean injunction to make new poems lively and energetic. The need for liveliness in poetic expression stands in the background even of poems in which Herbert seems to argue the contrary–the conclusion of 'Jordan (I)', for instance:

> I envie no mans nightingale or spring;
> Nor let them punish me with losse of ryme,
> Who plainly say, *My God, My King*. (ll. 12-14)

8 *The Art of English Poesy: A Critical Edition*, ed. Frank Whigham and Wayne A. Rebhorn (Ithaca and London: Cornell University Press, 2007), 133-34.

Simple, unadorned expression should be enough for devotion, just as the sonnet stripped to its bare form should be enough for poetry if it is devotionally heartfelt. But the phrase, '*My God, My King*', by itself, cannot be considered a poem because there is not enough to it. In isolation, it lacks the artistry necessary to move readers like the finest love poems. Indeed, its power here derives from the rest of 'Jordan (I)', which skillfully creates an affective identification between the speaking voice and the reader, thereby lending force to the simple declaration that provides a way out of the tensions between eloquence and honesty. The ensuing poem in *The Temple*, 'Employment (I)', plain in diction yet highly refined in its stanza construction and in the rhythm of its lines, implicitly shows there is more to 'turn[ing] delight into a sacrifice' than direct statements alone.

Something of the effort Herbert thought necessary for poetic eloquence is suggested in the second stanza of 'Jordan (II)', the *ars poetica* sequel to 'Jordan (I)', as Herbert describes his writing troubles:

> Thousands of notions in my brain did runne,
> Off'ring their service, if I were not sped:
> I often blotted what I had begunne;
> This was not quick enough, and that was dead.
> Nothing could seem too rich to clothe the sunne,
> Much lesse those joyes which trample on his head. (7-12)

These lines sketch a homely picture of Herbert's perfectionism, as he sorts through the '[t]housands of notions' in his 'brain' and 'often blot[s]' false starts. I am reminded of that later toiler and perfectionist W. B. Yeats, who describes the poet as 'never the bundle of accident and incoherence that sits down to breakfast' but rather as one who 'has been reborn as an idea, something intended, complete.'[9] The finished poem obscures the effort that went into achieving it. Most revealingly in 'Jordan (II)', line ten reveals what Herbert was looking for in a poetic line: 'This was not quick enough, and that was dead.' He wanted his lines to embody a sense of liveliness, a quickness, or in rhetorical terms, *energia*, which Sidney described as an essential 'forciblenesse' or energy capable of engaging the emotions of auditors. Roger Kuin recently has described Sidney as the central figure in positing both the theory and practice of *energia* as a fundamental criterion for effective, compelling poetry, the kind Donne and other members of his circle valued most.[10] Herbert's remark in line ten attests

9 Yeats, 'A General Introduction for My Work', *Essays and Introductions* (London: Macmillan, 1961), 30.

10 'Sustainable Energy: Philip Sidney and John Donne', *John Donne Journal* 33 (2014): 63-93.

to his acceptance of this criterion: the struggling poet looks for his lines to live and struggles because his attempts fail to achieve this necessary energy. Of course, the whispering voice at the end of 'Jordan (II)' criticizes the poet for struggling too hard ('*How wide is all this long pretence!*') and for investing too much ego in the process. But this development does not negate the criterion, especially when the last two lines ('*There is in love a sweetnesse readie penn'd:/Copie onely that, and save expense*') echo the conclusion of the first sonnet of *Astrophil and Stella*.

One feels the absence of Sidnean *energia* in the work of other religious sonneteers who similarly sought to strip the sonnet of the recognizable markers of the Petrarchan strain. These poets turned more completely away from courtly discourse in favor of other sources of discursive inspiration. Anne Lok, for example, wrote her sonnets in the vein of the Psalms. Her description of her sequence as a '*Paraphrase*' is quite accurate: the sequence proper is a verse-by-verse expansion of Psalm 51. Each of its twenty-one sonnets takes off from a different psalm verse, which is printed in the margin beside it as both gloss and guide. The psalm thus scripts each part of the meditation, as the 'penitent sinner' uses each verse to describe her offenses in general terms and to plead for mercy. It prevents the sonnets from making explicit connections with their secular counterparts. Even 'The preface, expressing the passioned minde of the penitent sinner', a five-sonnet introduction to the sequence, adopts the sorrowing, contrite language of the Psalms as opposed to the courtly elocutions of a Wyatt or a Surrey. And the entire work is quietly presented and carefully subordinated to Lok's translations of several of Jean Calvin's sermons on the song of Ezechias. She says of her own poems, 'I haue added this meditation folowying vnto the ende of this boke, not as parcel of maister Caluine's worke, but for that it well agreeth with the same argument, and was deliuered me by my frend with whom I knew might be so bolde to vse & publish it as pleased me.' That last remark seems disingenuous, given that 'A. L.' wrote the prefatory epistle to the volume as a whole and there claimed the sermon translations as her own, unless we are to think the 'I' who added the poems was the publisher and not the poet. Regardless of what we make of the last independent clause, publishing the sonnets is presented as an afterthought, and the poems themselves remain within the confines of established religious authorities. Anne Lok, in 1560, makes no claim for the originality of her sonnets as poetry to rival that of the secular poets, and there isn't any hint of what John Drury characterizes as Herbert's perfectionism with regard to eloquence.[11]

11 Drury, 139-51.

Three decades later, Anne Lok's son Henry Lok became the most prolific English religious sonneteer of the 1590s. His *Svndry Christian Passions Contained in two hundred Sonnets* (1593) and his *Svndry Affectionate Sonets of a Feeling Conscience* and *Pecular Prayers*, both of which were published in 1597, contain between them 328 sonnets, or more than one and a half times the number of Donne's surviving English poems and more than four times the number of lyrics in *The Temple*.[12] Meanwhile, Barnabe Barnes, Lok's contemporary, published his own *A Divine Centvrie of Spirituall Sonnets* in 1595. Together, Lok and Barnes account for more than half of the religious sonnets published in England during the 1590s.

Both poets occasionally invoke Petrarchan themes or situations in their poems: for example, in sonnet XVII of the second century of *Svndry Christian Passions*, Lok advances the idea of contrarieties to describe his spiritual suffering; in sonnets 6, 11, and 40 of his collection, Barnes pleas for God to look at him in a manner similar to that of a neglected lover. For the most part, though, both poets, like Anne Lok before them, eschew the discourse of lovers and courtiers in favor of a language that not only heavily references the Bible but also strives to imitate it. As Thomas Roche explains of Lok,

> All of the sonnets are richly adorned with allusions to figures in the Old and New Testaments. In fact, a reading of these poems creates a kaleidoscope sense of the Bible, impinging on the repentant soul on every side. In sonnet after sonnet one has the sense of the poet reaching out for God's grace through the collective history of other failures, other triumphs. 'These fragments I have shored against my ruin.' The total effect is powerful.[13]

Perhaps. But any power Lok's sonnets possess depends considerably on the reader's like engagement with the Bible rather than on the energy of Lok's expression. Similarly, Barnes' sonnets tend to work primarily within a web of Biblical allusiveness and give constant reminders (delivered parenthetically) of the Christian history that precipitates and justifies the speaker's acts of divine praise. A certain biblical deference guides the whole in both cases. Certainly Herbert–and Vaughan after him–is as deeply invested in the Bible as Lok or Barnes, if not more so, his Biblical allusiveness as extensive as theirs. But he and Vaughan more often than not are able to render received Biblical material

12 There are actually 204 sonnets in *Svndry Christian Passions*, counting the prefatory and conclusion sonnets of both centuries; 102 sonnets in *Svndry Affectionate Sonets*; and twenty-two sonnets in *Pecular Prayers*.

13 Roche, 158.

operational within poetic occasions as lively and immediate as any depicted in *Astrophil and Stella*. The same cannot be said of the prior sonneteers.[14]

Both poets tend to be overly didactic in method. More often than not, they directly present their moral themes rather than dramatize situations or interior movements that would appeal more strongly to readers. They often use theological terms to describe interior processes rather than reach for a more common idiom. They repeatedly invoke Biblical stories and images to situate the speaker and reader into the wide sweep of Christian history; but in doing so, they tend to sound as if they were worshipping in public rather than suffering in private. There is a kind of discursive orthodoxy throughout, as if they were somehow seeking public approval. Neither appears to have valued the Sidnean criterion of *energia* as assiduously as Herbert did, or if they did value it equally, they neglected to blot out enough lines to achieve it. This, in part, is why Herbert's sonnets sound so different from theirs. Herbert's voice remains perpetually his own. His sonnets sound more like his other poems than like any prior sonnet or biblical exemplars.

A comparison of how these poets handled the same technique *systrophe* (the piling on of images or ideas) for the purpose of definition illustrates this distinction clearly. Herbert's 'Prayer (I)', the fifth sonnet and nineteenth lyric in 'The Church', may well be one of the most famous definition poems in the English tradition of religious lyricism. The poem is especially known for the sense of wonder attending its speaker's attempt to capture the experience of prayer:

> Prayer the Churches banquet, Angels age,
> Gods breath in man returning to his birth,
> The soul in paraphrase, heart in pilgrimage,
> The Christian plummet sounding heav'n and earth;

14 Both Lok and Barnes wrote of their creative motivations in terms similar to Herbert's. Lok conceived of the writing of sonnets as a form of prayer and thought it

> good to set downe these abrupt passions of my passed afflictions, as witnesses of the impediments most stopping me in my Christian pilgrimage, and testimonies of the meanes of my evasion hitherto, which may serue for presidents for myself in the like future occasions: and not altogether vnprofitable for others to imitate.

As the last clause suggests, Lok published his sonnets out of a belief that they could be devotionally useful to readers. Barnes, who wrote his religious sonnets in France while in the employment of the Earl of Essex, explains that his poems similarly arose from his 'priuate motions' and the 'sting of divers wounds' that afflicted his soul as part of the 'combat betwixt earth and my spirit' (*A Divine Centurie of Spirituall Sonnets* [London: John Windet, 1595], A3). He believed they ought to be 'imployed to the propagation, honour, and mightinesse of [God's] Diuinitie'. Yet the sonnets of Lok and Barnes differ markedly from Herbert's in execution, see p. 3 of *Svndry Christian Passions* contained in two hundred sonnets (London: Richard Field, 1593).

Engine against th'Almightie, sinners towre,
Reversed thunder, Christ-side-piercing spear,
The six-daies world transposing in an houre,
A kinde of tune, which all things heare and feare;

Softnesse, and peace, and joy, and love, and blisse,
Exalted Manna, gladnesse of the best,
Heaven in ordinarie, man well drest,
The milkie way, the bird of Paradise,

Church-bels beyond the starres heard, the souls bloud,
The land of spices; something understood.

Herbert's adoption of this poetic device is not new. Lok's *Svndry Christian Passions* and Barnes' *A Divine Centvrie of Spirituall Sonnets* contain between them half a dozen definition poems that use *systrophe*. Moreover, in Welsh poetry, a similar device, called *dyafalu*, had a venerable history from the peak of the Welsh bards onward. Given his Welsh heritage, Herbert could well have known its Welsh incarnations. Four of Barnes' sonnets (32, 80, 84, and 85) adopt the same listing strategy. In perhaps his most accomplished, Sonnet 80, Barnes stacks images in a manner similar to 'Prayer (1)':

A Blast of winde, a momentary breath,
A watrie bubble simbolizde with ayre,
A sonne blowne Rose, but for a season fayre,
A ghostly glaunce, a skeleton of death,
A morning dew perling the grasse beneath,
Whose moisture Sunnes appearance doth impaire:
A lightning glimse: a Muse of thought and care:
A Planets shot; a shade which followeth:
A voice which vanisheth so soone as heard:
The thirstlesse heire of time: a rowling waue:
A shew no more in action then regard:
A Masse of dust: worlds momentary slaue
Is man in state of our olde Adam made,
Soone borne to die, soone flourishing to fade.[15]

15 The sonnets in Barnes' collection are printed in an italic typeface. Here, though, for ease of reading, I have removed the italics from the texts quoted.

A series of images (seventeen similitudes to Herbert's twenty-two) culminates in a conclusion meant to shake a reader into a new understanding of what is defined. In contrast to Herbert's poem, however, two features sap the potential of Barnes' sonnet to generate a compelling *energia*. First, Barnes does not maintain the same clarity of image that Herbert does. A few of his images are drawn from the world of experience (in keeping with the demands of verisimilitude, or *enargia*), and these images enable readers to meet those sections of the poem halfway: 'A Blast of winde', 'a momentary breath', 'A sonne blowne Rose', 'A morning dew perling the grasse beneath', 'A lightning glimse', and 'A voice which vanisheth so soone as heard'. The dew image is particularly effective because of the verb 'perling' and the inclusion of the 'grasse beneath', though by itself, dew, along with bubbles of various kinds, is one of the most conventional symbols for transience in all of early modern religious lyricism. But the other images not only are abstractions but also resist sensory identification. How are we to take 'a Muse of thought and care' or 'The thirstlesse heire of time' or 'A shew no more in action then regard'? Coming to these references, a reader has to stop to figure out what Barnes is trying to communicate.

To be sure, Herbert also uses abstractions; but he is careful to concretize them through figuration, and his metaphors carry an affective charge: 'Engine against th'Almightie, sinners towre,/Reversed thunder, Christ-side-piercing-spear,/The six-daies world transposing in an houre,/A kinde of tune, which all things heare and feare' (5 – 8). Sinners are trying to besiege God with medieval siege towers; they have found a way to reverse the direction of thunder; they re-pierce Christ's side with the emblematic spear of the centurion; their words create a music capable of inspiring fear. Surely, Richard Strier is correct when he observes, 'Herbert insists on the 'violence' here because he wants the contrast with traditional pictures of the harmony and tranquility of heaven to be as sharp as possible'.[16] Every similitude that strives in vain to capture the qualities and nature of prayer ploughs through a field of emotions. Herbert's chosen images are laden with emotional connotations; he intensifies these by revising conventional expectations. In 'reversed thunder', for example, 'we have a paradigm of poetic transformation: Herbert takes a biblical image, charged with ancient terror, works a small but significant change in it, and sends it off in a new direction'.[17] Even what may be the most abstruse–and therefore most heavily glossed–image, the 'six-daies world transposing in an houre', nonetheless

16 *Love Known: Theology and Experience in George Herbert's Poetry* (Chicago: University of Chicago Press, 1983), 187.

17 Chana Bloch, *Spelling the Word: George Herbert and the Bible* (Berkeley: University of California Press, 1985), 87.

roots itself in several highly relevant associations (the creation of the world, the recapitulation of a work week, transformed or reproduced in a 'different key from the original'[18] in an hour of prayer, perhaps during a Sunday liturgy). Herbert's clarity of reference and rich freight of emotional associations builds into an *energia* of marvel or wonder in the final lines.

But a second consideration also differentiates these two sonnets, a strategic choice at the outset of each poem. Barnes decided his poem would turn on a guessing game, an appeal to wit; that is, he decided to withhold as long as possible the term he sought to define. His assumption here must have been that the reader would play along and guess what all his images might amount to before discovering the correct answer in the last three lines: 'worlds momentary slaue/Is man in state of our olde Adam made,/Soone borne to die, soone flourishing to fade'. All the preceding images amount to a piecemeal definition of 'man', the moral of the story. This strategy of coyness, though it adheres to the workings of *systrophe*,[19] in this case also cannot help but introduce a distance, not an identification, between poet and reader, for the poet knows something the reader does not. As is typical with Barnes, the main effort of the poem is to convey a truth from the point of view of one who knows, not one who is discovering.

In sharp contrast, as Gary Kuchar explains, prayer, for Herbert, is 'more of a mode of discovery than a form of expression'.[20] Identification is the essence of the experience Herbert strives to capture. He not only immediately identifies the subject of his poem in the title, 'Prayer', but also he positions this 'Prayer' poem as the first in the series of poems so named. Additionally, to make certain he has his reader's full attention, he repeats 'Prayer' as the first word in the poem proper, as if to say, 'Let me offer you a definition of "prayer".' He wants no ambiguity whatsoever regarding the term defined. By resisting coyness, he maintains the overarching standard of clarity throughout his work. Equally important, he ensures his readers are following him, discovering along with him the intense associations of prayer and the earnestness or urgency with which the devout approach it. The latter effect is crucial for the poem's *energia*.

18 This is Helen Wilcox's gloss of "transposing," drawn from *OED* sense 7.

19 Richard A. Lanham, before quoting an example from Henry Peacham's *The Garden of Eloquence*, defines *systrophe* as 'Heaping up of descriptions of a thing without defining it' (*A Handlist of Rhetorical Terms*, 2nd edition [Berkeley: University of California Press, 1991], 149). That Herbert gives away the name of the thing described at the outset is consistent with *dyafalu*, however, which does not attach the same importance to an initial coyness.

20 *George Herbert and the Mystery of the Word* (Palgrave Macmillan, 2017), 106. This book was published after I wrote the original draft of this essay. My thanks to the anonymous reviewer who brought it to my attention.

At every moment he wants his reader to react both intellectually and emotionally to the dimension of prayer he highlights with every phrase. The wonder is that prayer can capture all of these associations simultaneously and nevertheless still be 'something understood', something not capable of all-encompassing definition. This honest admission would not have occurred to Lok or Barnes. They strive to eliminate, not allow for, indeterminacy. Barnes' poem settles into an easy didacticism; Herbert's risks mystery. Kuchar again: 'For Herbert, poetry and prayer are, in their very essence, means of hearkening to the invisible'.[21]

'Where is that Ancient Heat'?

From the beginning, Herbert seems to have realized, perhaps intuitively, that stripping the sonnet to its form alone would not suffice for eloquent poetry. The poet still labored under the burden to write authentic, fully realized, original poems energetic enough to engage the emotions of readers the way the most exciting love poets could. He must have been mindful that other near contemporaries, faced with the same implicit obligation, made a different choice when writing religious sonnets: rather than erase the Petrarch inheritance, they simply redirected some of its terms, thereby preserving the latent energy of desire and the emotional charges arising from its frustration. For example, Henry Constable's *Spirituall Sonnettes to the honour of God and hys Saintes* (ca. 1593) preserves many of the Petrarchan images and locutions; they now serve to describe the condition of the desiring Christian. Rather than address would-be mistresses, Constable directs poems to St. Katherine, St. Margaret, Mary Magdalene, and the Mother of Christ in the hopes that they might grant him the love of patrons interceding on his behalf for divine favor. William Alabaster's religious sonnets, composed during his period of struggling with Catholic conversion (1597-98), occasionally treat Christ as the object of love infusing the speaker of the poem with pain and longing.[22] And Donne's Holy Sonnets, which likely began circulating during the same period when Herbert first turned to writing poems (1609-10), frequently dramatize tortured emotions like those of one separated from his beloved. Each of these poets valued the energy reserves of the received sonnet heritage.

21 Kuchar, 242.

22 See, for example, sonnet 19, which begins 'Jesu, thy love within me is so main,/And my poor heart so narrow of content,/That with thy love my heart wellnigh is rent, . . .' (*The Sonnets of William Alabaster*. ed. G. M. Story and Helen Gardner [Oxford: Oxford University Press, 1959]).

Yet though he valued this same energy, Herbert was wary of its source: the sonnet's amorous ties.[23] He addresses this concern in the two 'New Year Sonnets,' especially the first, in which he expresses disgust that God has fared poorly as a rival of earthly men and women in contemporary love sonnets:

My God, where is that ancient heat towards thee,
Wherewith whole showls of *Martyrs* once did burn,
Besides their other flames. Doth Poetry
Wear *Venus* Livery? only serve her turn?
Why are not *Sonnets* made of thee? and layes
Upon thine Altar burnt? Cannot thy love
Heighten a spirit to sound out thy praise
As well as any she? Cannot thy *Dove*
Out-strip their *Cupid* easily in flight?
Or, since thy ways are deep, and still the same,
Will not a verse run smooth that bears thy name!
Why doth that fire, which by thy power and might
Each breast does feel, no braver fuel choose
Than that, which one day, Worms, may chance refuse.

As several critics have noted, these lines possess verbal parallels with some of Sidney's and Shakespeare's sonnets. Katherine Duncan-Jones sees in this poem and its sequel a 'shocked response' to the appearance of Shakespeare's *Sonnets* of 1609 and speculates that this publishing event might have precipitated Herbert's decision to 'embark on the programme of reclamation of secular poetic rhetoric that was to emerge as *The Temple*'.[24] Notice that Herbert begins

23 Strikingly, the downplaying of desire in his sonnets does not extend throughout Herbert's lyrics more generally. As is well-known, in some of his other poems, he invokes the logic of profane love to describe a desiring speaker like those encountered in Constable's and Donne's sonnets. In 'The Search', for example, the speaker is an abandoned lover desperately seeking the "Love" who has fled him. In 'Dulnesse', Herbert compares sexual virility and religious devotion to describe in physical terms his spiritual torpor. Similarly, the image of budding in 'The Flower' carries sexual overtones reminiscent of secular love poetry. In these and in other instances, Herbert explores some of the dimensions of spirituality through an implicit sensuality. 'In failing to acknowledge [Herbert's] eroticism and the uneasiness it arouses', as Michael C. Schoenfeldt remarks, 'we make Herbert's poetry the subject of our own repressions' (*Prayer and Power: George Herbert and Renaissance Courtship* [Chicago: University of Chicago Press, 1991], 231). Yet this undercurrent of eroticism elsewhere in *The Temple*, which scholars such as Schoenfeldt, Richard Strier, and others have noted (see, for instance, Strier, 89), does not extend to his formal sonnets.

24 *Shakespeare's Sonnets*, The Arden Shakespeare, Third Series [London: Thompson, 1997], 71. See also Malcolmson (3-6) for a discussion of intertextual connections with Sidney's sonnets. Joseph H. Summers sees Shakespearean connections in other sonnets. For example, he notes that

not by suggesting God has been neglected in poetry *per se* (even at sixteen he must have been aware of the numerous books of religious verse published between 1593 and 1609) but by marking a serious absence of the affective intensity true poetry requires: 'where is that ancient heat?' He speaks here of *energia*, assumed to issue from the passionate love that caused 'whole showls of Martyrs' to 'burn', psychologically and bodily, yet was curiously absent (in his view) from then current religious verse. An equivalent of this 'ancient heat' figures regularly in the poems of Sidney, Shakespeare, and presumably others, however, as a form of unfulfilled desire. This is why he asks, 'Doth Poetry/ Wear *Venus* Livery? only serve her turn?'. Strikingly, Herbert then suggests a program of rectifying the situation: 'Why are not *Sonnets* made of thee?' he asks, 'and layes/Upon thine Altar burnt?' The ensuing questions further suggest what a newly made religious poetry might look like: its inspiration (divine 'love') would be made manifest enough to 'Heighten a spirit to sound out' the poet's admiration as well as any love poet's; it would 'outstrip' its secular counterpart 'easily in flight'; and its style would be simple yet eloquent enough to convey the depth of a profound spirituality grounded in divine praise ('Or, since thy ways are deep, and still the same,/Will not a verse run smooth that bears thy name!') Given the power of divine inspiration and the ready and easy way with which it could fuel a new poetry, Herbert marvels why love poets invest their energies elsewhere in an overfondness towards corruptible flesh.

While these lines borrow '*Venus* Livery' (i.e., the references to vital spirits, Cupid, and love as an altar) in the act of nominally rejecting it, they also establish a significant departure from the modus operandi of the Sidnean or Shakespearean love sonnet in the disposition of their speakers. For, the poem is not so much an expression of the speaker's own 'ancient heat' toward God as it is an indignant criticism of a dereliction of duty among the poet's contemporaries. It evinces not an *energia* of lovesickness, the kind that emerges so easily from the pen of Alabaster who speaks of Jesus as a lover, or from that of Constable when he contemplates the Virgin Mary or St. Katharyne; rather, Herbert renders a (youthful) earnestness not predicated on Petrarchan amorousness.

Even in this earliest foray, Herbert the sonneteer assumes his 'pretty' rooms require the same decorum a proper person should expect in the common rooms of any well-run home. The same may be said of the second 'New Year Sonnet' as well. Here, too, we see the same indignation, the same earnestness, as the speaker marvels at the staggeringly misguided priorities of secular love poets.

'The Answer' is 'more personal than most of Herbert's poems; the speaker's experiences are not typical but individual, and more than any of the other sonnets, this poem suggests that Herbert may have read Shakespeare with profit' (*George Herbert: His Religion and Art* [Cambridge, MA: Harvard University Press, 1954], 183-84).

'[T]here is enough' in God 'to dry/Oceans of *Ink*', (1-2), he says; the roses and lilies speak God's praises; and yet poets trivialize them by comparing them to women's cheeks. Only near the end of the poem is there the slightest indication of the speaker's own possible 'heat' toward God:

Open the bones [of a woman], and you shall nothing find
  In the best *face* but *filth*, when Lord, in thee
  The *beauty* lies, in the *discovery*. (12-14)

Much might depend on how one reads '*discovery*.' But even so, this word is, at best, thin evidence of erotic desire. Missing here is that 'terrible longing for the absent and the unobtainable,' to borrow Anthony Low's description,[25] that is the primary focus of other religious sonneteers. Instead, the speaker desires not a love object but a gradual acceptance of divine service in whatever capacity God intends.

In writing the later sonnets, Herbert even more carefully avoided the diction of love poets. We can see this process occurring in his revisions of 'H. Baptisme (I)', which survives in two versions, an earlier one in the Williams manuscript and a final one in Bodleian MS Tanner 307 and in the finished *Temple*. From the start, this poem celebrates the redemptive powers of baptism. But the earlier draft speaks of this power in terms reminiscent of the love poets:

When backward on my sins I turne mine eyes
  And then beyond them all my Baptisme view
  As he y[t] Heaven beyond much thicket spyes
I pass y[e] shade & fixe vpon the true
Waters aboue y[e] Heavens. O sweet streams
  Yo[u] doe prevent most sins & for y[e] rest
  You give vs teares to wash them : lett those beams
W[ch] then ioin'd wth you still meet in my brest
And mend as rising starres & rivers doe. (1-9)

The 'streams' of baptism are 'sweet'; they provide cleansing 'tears' not altogether different from a lover's. Most notably, they merge with 'beams' within the speaker's 'brest'. This image recalls older theories of optics that the Petrarchists appropriated to render the emotional effects of being seen (or not) by one's actual or would-be beloved. The word carries this freight, even though Herbert's 'beams' in this

25 *Love's Architecture: Devotional Modes in Seventeenth-Century English Poetry* (New York: New York University Press, 1978), 12.

draft lack a clear referent. Does God's gaze create these beams? Are they merely beams of light from heaven? Regardless, they are meant to meet the baptismal waters in the speaker's 'brest' in a manner not unlike what happens when a beloved looks favorably upon a lovesick poet.

The last five lines depart from this amorous register in a series of images centered on measurement, repair work, and credit:

> In you Redemption measures all my tyme
> Spredding y[e] plaister equal to y[e] cryme
> You taught y[e] book of life my name, that so
> Whateuer future sinnes should mee mis-call
> Yo[r] first acquaintance might discredit all (10-14)

There is nothing explicitly Petrarchan here.

In the end, Herbert wanted nothing Petrarchan in the rest either, for, he substantially rewrote the first nine lines so that they accorded better with the last five:

> As he that sees a dark and shadie grove,
> Stayes not, but looks beyond it on the skie;
> So when I view my sinnes, mine eyes remove
> More backward still, and to that water flie,
>
> Which is above the heav'ns, whose spring and rent
> Is in my deare Redeemers pierced side.
> O blessed streams! either ye do prevent
> And stop our sinnes from growing thick and wide,
>
> Or else give tears to drown them, as they grow.
> In you Redemption measures all my time,
> And spreads the plaister equall to the crime:
> You taught the book of life my name, that so
>
> What ever future sinnes should me miscall,
> Your first acquaintance might discredit all.

Much has changed in this new version. The tone of the opening lines has become less urgent. Herbert has clarified the terms of his opening analogy and in the process draws less attention to the small movements of the speaker's gazing. He clarifies as well the source of Heaven's waters and in more obviously Christian terms: their 'spring and rent/Is my dear Redeemer's pierced side'. 'Sweet streams' becomes 'blessed streams', and gone are the 'beams' and the 'brest' wherein they mingle with waters. The notion of 'tears' remains, but Herbert has shifted more attention to the sins they drown by figuring sin as a kind of weed that can grow 'thick and wild' and the baptismal waters as a growth preventer or inhibitor. These new elements, the notion of sin's growth and the shift from washing to drowning, invoke more strongly the Continental literature of tears, long an outgrowth of traditional devotions centered on the figure of Mary Magdalene. The sonnet no longer sounds in any way like a love sonnet. Rather than seek a consummation with the divine, the speaker meditates on the effects of redemption on himself. This, too, is a sly adjustment of the self-interestedness of a Petrarchan speaker. Herbert's speaker views redemption as a 'plaister equall to' his many 'crimes' and takes comfort in the truth that because of Christ, 'What ever future sinnes should me miscall,/Your [Christ's] first acquaintance might discredit all' (13–4). This attitude differs markedly from Donne's in '*Crucifying*,' one of the sonnets in *La Corona*, where the speaker has such little faith he fears his parched soul will never find relief. Herbert's speaker suffers no such doubts. Nor does he indulge in suffering. Instead, he comports himself with the quiet stability of someone who knows what he is about in a manner not unlike Henry Lok's.

Such, I believe, is Herbert's intention, the creative challenge he set for himself: he wanted to salvage the sonnet from the service of profane love, to find other ways to charge it with emotion, and in the process, explore emotions other than those predominating in the Petrarchan mode. He wanted to retain the native power of the sonnet but without its illicit preoccupations. He wanted to move readers while he rendered, as accurately as possible, the interior life of one who has dedicated himself to divine service. This challenge nudged him into expanding the viable range of sonnet subjects to address dimensions of religious experience other than longing. Personalized or privatized desire gives way to critiques of materialistic fixations and the attitudes responsible for them ('The Sinner,' 'Avarice,' and 'Love [I]'); considerations of the affective character and tensions within the devotional life ('H. Baptisme [I]', 'Joseph's Coat,' Sinne [I],' and 'The Answer'); considerations of spiritual education ('Love [II], 'The H. Scriptures [I] and [II],' and 'The Sonne'); parables of divine service ('Christmas,' 'Redemption' and 'The Holdfast'); and an unforgettable expostulation on the experiential qualities of prayer ('Prayer [I]'). This refashioning, like so many other refashionings in *The Temple*, confirms an essential truth about Herbert the poet: 'He did not pursue novelty for its own sake; rather, he sought to transform and revitalize the conventional so as to make it freshly available to serious poetry'.[26] Rather

26 Summers, 171.

than pursue the fulfillment of desire, the speakers of such poems as 'Redemption' and 'The Holdfast' seek the 'new small-rented lease' that would make 'all things' 'more [theirs] by being [Christ's]' ('Redemption', 4; 'The Holdfast', 12). They seek to give up themselves for others. Two decades later, Milton would espouse a similar vision of service through the sonnet, though not with a similar construction of domesticity foregrounded. Nevertheless, we see in his and in Herbert's sonnets how far the religious sonnet opened to a variety of nonamorous concerns during more than half a century.

Kestrels
by Colin See-Paynton

RIC HOOL

Things You Learn in Scouts

for Malcolm Coe

It remains imprinted these years distant
that innocent New Year's Eve,
the house doors left open and you
showing me how to knock back whisky,
choking and spluttering, tears erupting
from eyes; golden alcohol
hosing from your nose.

Another time, caught in mist
on Helvellyn retreating hunched-down
for fear of falling. How
coldly we camped that night
sleepless and homesick. I am

waving Malcolm from a time
we never imagined would arrive. Waving
across milestones, children and jobs – yours
on a North Sea platform and mine
by way of muse and music - beyond
the bay; behind the breakwaters of childhood.
We crashed through adulthood's jungle.

Flicking this semaphore, "Did you
ever think we'd get this far?"

PRUE CHAMBERLAYNE

A Different Anchoring of Love

Immersed in backwash from his seizure
from the living, we walk the Cardiff Bar,
dredge the less-said, things out of reach.

Choppy high tide, water wrestling
with itself held and funnelled
between here and Somerset;
beyond slate-grey it blooms incarnadine,

spreading rich as menstrual blood,
fecundity swept down from marshes
of Plynlimon, red marl of Shrewsbury,
wooded valleys of the Wye

also delivering, silt leached out
in horrifying quantities,
millennia of soil seepage,
carving by water – were mountains higher?

Sediment-suspended-sparkle in the lapping –
iron avenue of porphyry
that lured in traders, ships waiting
to ride the tide in channel torrents.

West winds and currents bring the spent
back in, re-plaster banks
and ledges; even here we watch
leather mudflats nudged at ebb.

Elvers and salmon manage the crossing
from sour to sweet and back again,
traversal Tristan and Isolde knew,
these plunging waves that heaved and hurled

the Cornish cliffs confronting them,
the flood of words they'd been denying
unleashed in terrifying passion.

B. J. BUCKLEY

Along Goose Creek

That man out there, up to his knees in water
unconcerned, is fishing. The nylon filament
he casts out like a spider flinging web
catches on air, shifts, floats, settles
like cob silk on a mirror. The fly
whose perfect mimicry a perfect cast ensures

settles too, waits, lifts again a moment later.
The man is himself a liquid element,
quicksilver shining in his bones. He grabs
air fish-mouthed, brushes nettles
and marsh wort carefully aside, scans sky
for rain. He thinks of open doors –

cool hollows under the cutbank, and the old laughter
of fish outsmarting men. When God divided firmaments
one from the other, and made the drab
brown of earth and gave it over, some souls battled
back to sea, to rivers, to the sigh
of light on mobile surfaces. They endured,

and now this man, born so long after,
carries his water-soul like a penitent
up into the pine hills. Blue pebbles
polished round as river stones settle
into the deep sockets of his eyes,
and his blood, burnt pure

in the heat of the afternoon, batters
the deep channels of his heart. Intent
and careful, his quick wrist guides the ebb
and flowing of the line, the fly, unfolding petals
of his trap, until some fish not capable of asking why
or how accepts deception, takes the lure.

At morning and evening the man in tatters
of a favorite shirt moves up the creek and down, bent
the way a willow's bent by treble
currents: water, wind, desire. Birds rattle
and cry up out of sleep as the man walks, shy
as an egret, as practised, and as sure.

Equinox

Wind from the western
quarter – its fragrance – dryness,
emptiness, the waving grass.
Antelope scat.
A little blood, where rabbit
fed coyote,
where mouse fed hawk.
Lost perfumes, too,
unfallen rain, dried-up
waterholes, sharp alkali
from low corners
of stubbled fields.
In the nose of fox,
kaleidoscope scent:
cock pheasants
rattling up from the ditches
to leave, unprotected,
two covert hens.
And then there is the burning,
the waste corn disced under,
ash sifting down
from every breeze.
What else is left
for the heart to want?
Low sun, rising moon, sere leaves
of the windbreak,
all the colours
of fire.

WILLIAM VIRGIL DAVIS

Hopper's "Automat"

A woman is sitting at a white-
topped table in an emptied room.
She wears a glove on one hand
and is holding a cup of coffee
in the other, staring into it. Her
head is hooded in a helmet-like
hat pulled down around her ears.
Her green coat, with rich black
velvet cuffs and collar, is open,
exposing her low-cut dress.
Her crossed legs are cut off at
the knees by the table top. On
the window sill behind her is a
bowl of fallen fruit. There is a
period heating unit to one side,
near the door. Above her, in the
darkened window, a doubled trail
of globe-like lights diminish
into dark and nothingness. The
woman seems to be oblivious
to everything, seems sad or
disappointed, somewhere far
away, waiting, like Piper Laurie
in an empty lunchroom, for
Paul Newman to find her there.

Poem Beginning with a Sentence from Stevens

We sit listening to music as in an imagination
in which we believe. What can we know?
The music means what we want it to mean
and we believe that that is what we know.

All afternoon the rain rains down the windows
and the cat, curled on her cushion, watches
it intermittently, between wakings and naps.

The music blends into the afternoon, like rain
on windows, and we, watching like the cat
does, nod in and out of our thoughts and
recreate what we know as music in our minds.

PAMELA COREN

Pressure

Storm coming close: heat wrings out the air. Stillness.
Cloud blackens and builds: it could sweep you off the hillside
however you close the doors, unplug the gadgets,
however carefully you cut the apples for pudding
and set out the quiet dinner. It will not stop.
The dog's afraid, and clings. Storm's in her bones,
cracked under the falling tree.

See what my rivers do to escape me
when I drown them in their beds.
Air sags and breaks under my weight.
Night-black now, rodded with rain.
You can no more stop it than the bombers
arming at the air-base. The dull submarine
in its weight noses out of the corporate dark.

ALISON BRACKENBURY

The Third

Unwanted, yet he came
through cat flaps; hissed; would bite
to bone. Feet marred his past.
They kicked him out of fear.

Damage too deep to name
sinks, purring. Eyes by night
dazzle to blue of vast
seas which have shed all ice.

After the Rain

Two crows sit hunched in conference.
This does not touch me in my heated sett
where I stroke my wounded ankle, gently,
where I gaze into half-drowned light.
It is bad news if you are small, quick, wet,
if you need to eat before night.

GRAHAM HARTHILL

Crusader

A boy of 14, in
shitty breeches – strappings
of bullock-leather, a bit of
a red rag for a hat

wide-eyed,
squeezed
between oaken cattle-stall and
rocky edge of
poor Patricio's fields

his head a rhyme
of God's
light:
if God himself says
Come,
there can be no fear in it

only fame,
and stretching his marvellous veins
outside this foggy bowl
his mind already beginning to drip
with perfumed towns
and girls, and
other bloods

CHARLES WILKINSON

Pocket of Loss

The pace of day debits
light from the balance
of dusk. Accelerated
to the end, how much
have we kept in hand?
Here is our small change:
moments, mostly spent,
for what was proffered
went & can never
be rebated. The worth
of remembrance may
be debased, yet a knot
in the handkerchief
reminds of the hours
of tanners & crowns:
all sides now effaced.
Once the lining's gone
there is an absence
of silver & lace,
for the loss is worse
when walking, as coins
slip down to the ground.
Grief's metal has no echo
on moss, & returning
never finds the place.

JOSEPHINE SCOTT

The End of the Season

The hammer in the clock tower
strikes a short dull note,
I do not like these dark mornings
that are as warm as midday.

A cock crows as the sky lightens,
revealing a stone cross
growing out of a field,
as though expelled from the earth.

At the bottom of the pool
a dead spider clings
to a bougainvillea flower,
thin legs scrunched in pain.

The water in the harbour
is the colour of a bruise.
A harsh breeze rustles the palms like raffia,
the air crackles with your energy.

I'm glad to be leaving this tired place,
empty streets with shuttered windows,
awnings curled like furled umbrellas.
Then by the road I glimpse

five carousel horses standing side by side,
their bowed heads draped with sackcloth,
startling penitents.

Brilliana Harley: Civil War Woman

VICKI KAY

The lives and writings of the seventeenth-century Vaughan brothers, Henry and Thomas, are inseparably bound to issues engendered by their experiences of the English Civil War (1642-1651). The trials endured by the two men are widely known to readers of *Scintilla,* whereas those of their contemporary, Lady Brilliana Harley, may not be. This article seeks to introduce the Civil War experiences of Harley, whose own letters survive to tell her tale, and so shed light on the wider history of Civil War lives. Shifting the location of writing from the Vaughans' Usk valley to Harley's Herefordshire (though both, of course, are in the Marches), the gender of the author from male to female, and the political side from Royalist to Parliamentarian, provides a different angle and perspective to those familiar with the Vaughans. Whether this drastically changes perceptions and presentations of devotion, family life, finance and indeed the War itself, can be decided by the reader.

Named after the Dutch town of Brill, where her father was lieutenant-governor at the time of her birth, Brilliana was baptised in 1598. She was the second daughter of Edward, Viscount Conway and Viscount Killutagh (d.1631), of Ragley, Warwickshire, and his wife Dorothy (d.1612), who was herself daughter of Sir John Tracy of Gloucestershire.[1] Brilliana and her siblings were naturalised by a private act of parliament in 1606. In July 1623, Brilliana became the third wife of Sir Robert Harley (bap.1579-d.1656) of Brampton Bryan, Herefordshire. Lady Brilliana and Sir Robert Harley had seven children: Edward (1624-1700), Robert (1626-1673), Thomas (b.1628), Brilliana (b.1629), Dorothy (b.1630), Margaret (b.1631), and Elizabeth (b.1634). Elizabeth was the only child not to survive into adulthood. During the Civil War, Lady Brilliana Harley defended the family estate of Brampton Bryan whilst her husband and eldest son were away fighting for the Parliamentarian side; she followed the wishes of her

1 Oxford Dictionary of National Biography http://www.oxforddnb.com.ezproxy.bangor.ac.uk/view/10.1093/ref:odnb/9780198614128.001.0001/odnb-9780198614128-e-12334?rskey=6d6oMU&result=1 [Accessed 31 October 2018]. All biographical information is from this source, unless otherwise indicated.

husband, despite her own desire to move to a place of safety. The Harleys were Puritan supporters of the Parliamentarian cause, notwithstanding their location in Herefordshire which was a Royalist stronghold. Lady Brilliana's surviving letters to her husband and eldest son demonstrate her piety as well as her astute management of the family affairs. She not only communicates the local political situation to Sir Robert and Ned, but also sends packages of food and medicine with her letters. She successfully resisted the Royalist siege of Brampton Bryan which began 26 July 1643 and lasted almost seven weeks, ending on 9 September.[2]

During February 1643, Harley had received a summons from Fitzwilliam Coningsby, Governor of Hereford, to surrender the castle, its men and munitions, to the use of the King; she refused, claiming that she merely had the equipment required to defend her house which was her lawful right. Coningsby's successor, William Vavasour, took action in an attempt to force Harley into submission on 26 July by surrounding Brampton Bryan with 'two or three troops of horse, closely followed by two or three hundred foot soldiers' which cut off all access to and from the estate.[3] Musket fire ensued, earthworks were built, the estate cattle and sheep were driven away, and the parish church, in close proximity to the gates of the castle, was won by the besieging Royalist forces. Harley protested her loyalty to the King claiming she was doing nothing more than lawfully protecting her property and continued to delay negotiations with Vavasour through ingeniously playing upon her rank and gender, presenting herself as a weak woman who could not act without the instruction of her husband. Whilst some inhabitants of the castle were injured, including Harley's friend, Lady Colebourn who lost an eye thanks to a bullet, the casualties seem to have been few. Finally, on 9 September, the troops besieging Brampton Bryan were called away to the greater task of the battle at Gloucester, where the Royalist siege had been lifted. Harley died on 29 October 1643 at Brampton Bryan, shortly after sending her final letter, whilst anticipating further Royalist attack.

Approximately 375 letters written by Lady Brilliana Harley survive, mainly to her husband (from 1623) and to her son, Ned (from 1638) until her death in October 1643. Of the surviving collection, 115 are autograph, with the remaining 260 making use of a scribe, occasionally her younger son, Thomas. For early modern society, the use of a scribe could be an assertion of social status, as well as a strategy to speed up the laborious, and messy, writing

2 Rachel Adcock, Sara Read and Anna Ziomeck ed., *Flesh and Spirit: An Anthology of Seventeenth-Century Women's writing* (Manchester: Manchester University Press, 2014), p. 125; Alison Plowden, *Women All on Fire: The Women of the English Civil War* (Stroud: Sutton Publishing, 1998), pp. 53-9. All following details of the siege are informed by Plowden, unless otherwise indicated.

3 Plowden, p.53.

process. In a study of early modern women's letter-writing, James Daybell has explained,

> Engulfed by business and legal affairs arising from estate and household management, women were responsible for large amounts of out-going correspondence [. . .] It was therefore only administrative good sense to employ a scribe to deal with what potentially could be an overwhelming amount of paperwork.[4]

The use of a scribe did not mean that a woman was unable to write her own letters, nor did it deny her authorship; rather, it is evidence of her time-management and administrative role as mistress of a household. Owing to their ability to produce documents quickly, professional scribes were used for personal as well as business correspondence.[5] Despite clearly being literate (in Latin and French as well as English), Harley uses idiosyncratic spelling in those letters written in her own hand. Her letters give evidence of the practicalities faced by a woman running an estate both in the absence of her husband and dealing with the imminent danger of civil war. Sara Mendelson and Patricia Crawford have argued that, during the Civil War, 'wives' work in estate management intensified' as more husbands were away from home than during peacetime.[6] Harley's letters certainly seem to support this argument. As letters, the texts written by Harley make the journey from the domestic household into the public arena. The exchanges between Harley, at home, and her husband and son studying in Oxford, in London on business, and at war, show their author to be concerned with far more than the domestic 'female' concerns of raising children and governing the home. Indeed, Jennifer Summit has argued that early modern women's epistolary writing was 'not in opposition to women's household activities but in tandem with them taking its place as a female 'accomplishment' alongside the domestic practices of needlework and cookery.'[7] Harley's writing proves her to be an adept correspondent as well as deputy estate manager.

4 James Daybell, 'Female Literacy and the Social Conventions of Women's Letter-Writing in England, 1540-1603', in *Early Modern Women's Letter Writing, 1450-1700*, ed. by James Daybell (Basingstoke: Palgrave, 2001), pp. 59-76 (p. 65).

5 Daybell, 'Female Literarcy', p. 65.

6 Sara Mendelson and Patricia Crawford, *Women in Early Modern England 1550-1720* (Oxford: Clarendon Press, 1998), p. 310.

7 Jennifer Summit, 'Writing Home: Hannah Woley, the Oxinden Letters, and Household Epistolary Practice', in *Women, Property and the Letters of the Law in Early Modern England*, ed. by Nancey E. Wright, Margaret W. Ferguson and A.R. Buck (Toronto: University of Toronto Press, 2004), pp. 201-18 (p. 202).

In her letters, Lady Brilliana Harley can be seen defending the family home against the threat of Royalist attack, and indeed in the event of the siege outlined above. In the absence of her husband and eldest son, Harley becomes more than their second-in-command: she effectively becomes the commander of a Brampton Bryan garrison. James Daybell has noted that 'the kind of news conveyed in women's correspondence illustrates female interest in areas of news traditionally viewed as 'masculine': parliamentary business, war, armed rebellions.'[8] Harley's letters go further than showing an interest: they show the practicalities of defending an estate from siege during the Civil War. Her letters go beyond 'female interest'; they are created out of necessity and direct involvement with war, and showcase capabilities fitting of the leader of her own estate-based army. Harley requests and receives weapons in numerous letters, including muskets, bandoliers (belts worn over the shoulder to hold both muskets and ammunition), powder and match.[9] As well as ordering weapons for her own use, Harley supplies these means of war to the Parliamentarian forces through deliveries to her son and husband which accompany her correspondence. In a letter to Ned dated 24 June 1642 she refers to 'the 2 pistolls you rwite [sic] me word your father would haue' which she sends along with the letter (p. 172).

Interestingly, Harley desires advice from her husband on defending Brampton Bryan, but refers to the castle as *hers* rather than theirs or his, suggesting that she feels responsible for, and entitled to claim ownership of, the estate since she has been left as deputy in a dangerous situation: 'I hope your father will giue me full derections how I may best haue *my* howes gareded, if need be' (p. 180, my emphasis). Perhaps Harley interprets her husband's action of leaving her at Brampton Bryan as a partial-relinquishment of control; she is now in charge whether she/he likes it or not. Indeed, Harley explicitly states to Ned that she is not happy remaining amidst a Royalist stronghold:

> I acknowledg I doo not thinke meself safe wheare I am. I loos the comfort of your fathers company, and am in but littell safety, but that my trust is in God; and what is doun in your fathers estate pleasess him not [. . .] but if your father thinke it beest for me to be in the country, I am every well pleased with what he shall thinke beest. (p. 167)

8 James Daybell, *Women Letter-Writers in Tudor England* (Oxford: Oxford University Press, 2006), p. 156.

9 Brilliana Harley, in *Letters of the Lady Brilliana Harley, wife of Sir Robert Harley, of Brampton Bryan, Knight of the Bath. With Introduction and Notes by Thomas Taylor Lewis, A.M. vicar of Bridstow, Herefordshire* (London: Camden Society, 1853), pp. 153-4; p. 161; p. 178; p. 183. All references are to this edition of Harley's letters, hereafter cited by page number.

Harley is intensely aware of the danger she faces as a Parliamentarian supporter living within a Royalist county. However, she fulfils her marriage vows to obey her husband and remains on the estate to act as his representative, taking comfort in her devotion; the discord on the Harleys' land will certainly displease God. A later letter to Ned, written on 20 June 1642, reiterates her feelings:

> Since your father thinkes Hearefordsheare as safe as any other country, I will thinke so too; but when I considered how long I had bine from him, and how this country was affected, my desire to see your father, and my care to be in a place of safety, made me ernestly desire to come vp to Loundoun; but since it is not your father's will, I will lay aside that desire. (p. 170).

Harley obeys her husband's orders to remain at Brampton Bryan despite her fears for the family's safety and despite her desire to be with him. The difference between male freedom of movement and female restriction is acutely apparent in Harley's letters.

The business of war impacts on the very form of the letters that Harley writes from Brampton Bryan. Gary Schneider has highlighted the 'difficulties of epistolary communication' in the early modern period, such as 'the threat of miscarriage, interception, and misinterpretation', and this is particularly pertinent to Harley's Civil War communications.[10] From March 1642 onwards, a number of Harley's letters are written in a code which is broken with a key of cut paper which is placed over the letter (pp. 191-4; pp. 196-7; p. 199). The openings in the cut paper create sensible sentences to convey her message; without the key, the letters appear to be jumbled words of nonsense. She gives keys to Ned and her daughter, Brill. Harley's invention adapts her writing to fit the dangerous political situation of the Civil War: she occupies a precarious position as a Puritan, female, Parliamentarian supporter within the Royalist county of Herefordshire. Under such circumstances, Harley's letter-writing becomes a defiant act of ingenuity.

Harley's letters demonstrate her role in financing the Parliamentarian cause. In January 1642 she counsels Ned on the best way to raise funds for their war effort:

> in my opinion it weare better to borrow mony, if your father will giue any, then to giue his plate; for we doo not know what straits we may be put to, and thearefore I thinke it is better to borrow whillst on may, and keepe the plate for a time of neede [. . .] This I doo not say, that I am

10 Gary Schneider, 'Affecting correspondences: body, behavior, and the textualization of emotion in early modern English letters', *Prose Studies*, 23.3 (2000), 31-62 (p. 32).

> vnwilling to part with the plate or any thing ells in this case: if your father cannot borrow mony, I thinke I might finde out some in the cuntry to lend him some. (p.169)

Harley encourages Ned to suggest to his father that, if he wants to donate money to the Parliamentarian cause, he would be better borrowing cash rather than giving the family plate. She sensibly suspects that the situation is volatile and unpredictable and so plans to save the plate as an insurance policy should they need money to survive in the coming months and years of the war. The wills of Maud Parr (1530) and Elizabeth Hardwick (1601) also show a similar concern with investing family wealth in plate. These early modern women understand that plate has greater stability as an investment than ready money. Harley is keen to stress that she is not reluctant to part with the family possessions for the greater good, however. She offers to act as in intermediary to obtain credit for her husband, showing female involvement in the financing of warfare.

Six months after recommending that Sir Robert and Ned donate cash funds to the Parliamentarian cause, Harley sends the plate. In July 1642, she writes to Ned, 'I am confident you are not troubled to see the plate goo this way; for I trust in our gratious God, you will haue the frute of it' (p. 177). Presumably they can no longer borrow money and so must cash-in their assets. Mendelson and Crawford have noted that both Parliamentarian and Royalist supporters, men and women, raised funds by donating plate, cash and jewellery.[11] Antonia Fraser points out that London women sold their jewellery at the Guildhall to raise funds for the Parliamentary forces, whilst others in London, Norwich, Canterbury, and Coventry organised committees to raise money for horses and troops.[12] In his mock-heroic narrative poem, *Hudibras*, in the 1660s Samuel Butler would recall women, 'From *Ladies* down to *Oyster-Wenches*' and '*Handmaids* of the *City*', financing the Civil War:

> *Women*, that left no stone unturn'd,
> In which the *Cause* might be concern'd:
> Brought in their children's *spoons* and *whistles*,
> To purchase *Swords, Carbines* and *Pistols* [. . .]
> All they could rap and run and pilfer,
> To scraps, and ends of Gold and Silver [. . .][13]

11 Mendelson and Crawford, p. 401.

12 Antonia Fraser, *The Weaker Vessel: women's lot in seventeenth-century England* (London: Weidenfeld and Nicolson, 1984), p. 185.

13 Samuel Butler, *Hudibras*, ed. by John Wilders (Oxford: Clarendon Press, 1967), pp. 148-9, ll.777-809.

Butler depicts, and mocks, women across the social ranks cashing in their assets, like Lady Brilliana Harley, in order to support their cause. The Harleys' plate would form part of Ned's inheritance, yet his mother suggests that it will act as an investment to bear 'frute' of a greater inheritance: political stability and Puritan victory. 'Frute' suggests a multiplying and a reproduction connected with labour – both manual labour and the labouring of birth. The Parliamentarian fight is one which Harley hopes will give birth to a better future for her family and England as a whole.

Along with the delivery of plate, Harley sends food: 'In the hamper with the plate, I haue sent your father a cake; it whas sent me this morning' (p. 177). Throughout her letters she mentions parcels of food and drink for Ned and her husband which accompany her writings. Prior to the Civil War, when Ned was studying at Oxford, Harley wrote to him, 'I haue sent you some juice of licorich, which you may keepe to make vse of, if you should haue a coold.' (p. 9). Harley's motherly and wifely duty to provide nourishment for her family is not stopped by the need to fund warfare; indeed, the two duties coexist in her writing.

As well as pistols, plate, food, and drink, Brilliana Harley sends a man and a horse to join Ned's 'troope' in May 1643, 'becaus I cannot be with you myself' (p. 199). As a woman, Harley is unable to take up arms and fight as part of the Parliamentarian army and so she sends a man in her place, fighting by proxy. Harley employs a deputy to fight in her place in the same way that her husband instructs her to defend and administer the Brampton Bryan estates as his deputy at home. She informs Ned that 'the hors cost me 8*l*' (p. 199). The National Archives Currency Converter confirms that £8 in 1642 would purchase one horse and is equivalent to £940 today.[14] This amount could also pay the wages of a skilled tradesman in the mid-seventeenth century for 114 days; horses were clearly a valuable commodity as a means of transport, of labour, and of war. Two months later, in July 1643, Harley writes to Ned that she 'can get but little towards the byeing of a hors, what it is, I haue sent you inclosed' (p. 207). Due to the siege of Brampton Bryan she can no longer afford to buy a horse outright, nor does she have the opportunity to do so, confined to the property and with retail and supply lines cut off.[15] Her letters are abundant in examples of her involvement in financing warfare precisely because of the historical moment in which she wrote. Had her letters been written in peacetime it is unlikely that she would have been so vocal in advising her husband and son on how best to

14 The National Archives Currency Converter <http://www.nationalarchives.gov.uk/currency-converter/#currency-result> [Accessed 14 January 2019].

15 The siege began in July 1643 and lasted for six weeks.

support a military cause, had the letters existed at all: it is the absence of her son and husband that gives occasion to Harley's writing. Her social as well a political position allows her to become a participant in the financial side of warfare: for her it provides a satisfying alternative to personally taking up arms to fight.

Amidst her practical concerns for defending Brampton Bryan, Brilliana Harley's letters demonstrate her piety. She sends money to her son, Ned, in January 1638 so that he can give alms: 'I haue sent you a littell purs with some smale mony in it, all the pence I had, that you may haue a penny to giue a power [poor] body [person]' (p. 20). Puritan acts of charity were not performed in the hope or expectation of 'earning' salvation, as was much Catholic almsgiving, but to demonstrate their place as one of the chosen elect, and as a performance of Christian duty in their position as the children of God.[16] In the same letter to Ned, in the very sentence before mentioning the purse of money for the poor, Harley requests her son's opinion on 'some part of Mr. Caluin' he has 'reed', desiring him to 'send [. . .] word how you like him' (p. 20). Harley's eagerness to discuss Calvin's writings with her son suggests she values his opinion whilst also hinting at her own affinity to Calvin's beliefs and her role as a consumer of devotional texts. Harley writes of devotion and money with equal ease, switching from one to another in such a way that implies the two are vital parts of her understanding of the world and that she does not see them to be in opposition. Indeed, in December 1638, Harley's letter to Ned illustrates her ability to use mercantile metaphors adeptly in her discussion of religion:

> I blles my God, for thos good desire you haue, and the comfort you finde in the sarfeing your God. Be confident, he is the best Master, and will giue the beest waiges, and they weare the beest liuery, the garment of holyness, a clotheing which neuer shall weare out, but is renwed euery day. (p. 16)

Harley encourages Ned to be pious, and uses commercial metaphors to do so. God is presented as an employer and provider of wages and livery. Of course, the parable of the labourers in the vineyard being rewarded for their spiritual toil would be familiar to Harley and Ned (Matthew 20:1-16). Similarly, they would be aware of the parable of the wedding guests with the significant 'garment of holiness', along with St Paul's call to 'Put on the whole armour of

16 Helen Wilcox, 'Sacred and Secular Love: 'I Will Lament, and Love'', in *The Oxford Handbook of Early Modern English Literature and Religion* ed. by Andrew Hiscock and Helen Wilcox (Oxford: Oxford University Press, 2017), pp. 613-33 (p. 620).

God, that ye may be able to stand against the wiles of the devil' (Matthew 22:1-14; Ephesians 6:11). Without doubt, Harley's letter is informed by these Biblical teachings. Her language recalls that of the medieval pilgrim Margery Kempe who uses legal metaphors in the presentation of her relationship with Christ, naming him the executor of her good works.[17] Both Harley and Kempe understand and present their relationships with Christ as contractual and reciprocal; they will receive a heavenly return for their true devotion. This idea of spiritual reward for pious and virtuous lives runs throughout medieval and early modern women's writing, regardless of whether the authors are Catholic or Protestant. Such a theme also features in the writing of men of this period, however, this sense of belonging to God seems particularly pertinent to women, perhaps due to their worldly positions in which they 'belonged' to men; first to their fathers, and then to their husbands.

Harley's piety informs her perception of the family's role in the Civil War. She interprets her family's actions as their godly duty; it is for God that they take up arms for the Parliamentarian cause. In July 1642 Harley informs her son of the tense situation in Herefordshire:

> deare Ned, I hope you and myself will remember for whous caus your father and we are hated. It is for the caus of our God, and I hope we shall be so fare from being ashamed of it or trubelled, that we beare the reproche of it, that we shall binde it as a crowne upon us; and I am confident the Lord will rescue His chillderen from reproche. (p. 179)

It is clear that Harley feels victimised and ostracised by her Herefordshire neighbours as a result of the family's Parliamentarian support, claiming that Harleys are 'hated'. However, she takes comfort in her belief that the family support 'the caus of our God' and so they should neither be 'ashamed' nor face Divine 'reproche'. She suggests that the Harley family should take the hatred and reproach from their contemporaries and 'binde it as a crowne upon us', recalling Christ's crown of thorns and transforming their suffering into evidence of their own position as children of God. Evidently Harley gains a sense of righteousness and comfort through her devotion and conviction that the Parliamentarian cause is favoured by God. Harley's faith gives her the necessary strength and optimism to face the adversity of being an isolated, Parliamentarian, woman in a county of Royalist supporters.

17 'Lord, sythen thow hast foryovyn me my synne, I make the myn executor of alle the god werkys that thow werkyst in me.' Margery Kempe, *The Book of Margery Kempe*, ed. by Barry Windeatt (Cambridge: D.S. Brewer, 2004), p. 81, ll.633-5.

In Harley's final letter before her death in October 1643, she writes to Ned, who is now 'Colonell Harley' of the Parliamentarian forces, that she hopes 'the Lord will deleuer me' both from a potential second siege, and from the 'very greate coold' from which she is suffering (p. 209). Harley wishes that 'the Lord will be mercifull to me, in giuing me my health, for it is an ill time to be sike in' (p.209). For Harley, her faith in God's help is a component of her pragmatism. She writes of the illness which will prove fatal in a matter of days, yet in this letter she presents it as an inconvenience: she does not have time to be sick. If she is unwell, Harley anticipates with great practical common sense that she will not be useful in the defence or administration of the estate, perhaps wondering who will take her place as letter-writer and estate commander. It is also possibly an 'ill time to be sike in' if the castle is once again under siege by the 'souldiers come to Lemster and 3 troopes of hors to Heariford with Sr William Vauasor' meaning to 'viset Brompton againe', as Harley will not be able to obtain medicine or the services of a doctor from outside her home (p. 209). It is also plausible that the financial cost of defence means that she cannot afford to pay for either of these. The hope and practicality of Harley's final letter heightens its poignancy: she died on 29 October 1643 at Brampton Bryan, just twenty days after sending her final letter to Ned. The castle was still preparing to face a second siege.

In this brief discussion of Lady Brilliana Harley's Civil-War letters, we have caught a glimpse of the chaotic and terrifying ways in which one seventeenth-century woman's life was changed by the political turmoil. The events of the Civil War period, which brought such distress and loss to the Vaughans, provided Harley with opportunities to act with more autonomy than she may ever have experienced in peacetime. Despite the fear that Harley felt at being vulnerably placed within a Royalist county without the protection of her husband and her eldest son – an anxiety that reveals itself regularly in the correspondence – the overriding sense of her character is one of calm strength, secure in the belief that God will reward the toil and suffering of her family. Harley's devotion is key to her interpretation of life, and the uniting force of her Civil War actions. Throughout her letters Harley remains acutely aware of what she perceives to be her duty as wife and mother; indeed, it is this duty to act on behalf of the family and to provide care for them, along with her belief in God, that allows her to write so forcefully and exhibit such fortitude in her Civil-War correspondence. Paradoxically, Harley's obedience to her husband and to God led her to break most of the restrictions on women of her generation: it enabled her to run an estate, make decisions and advise her husband on financial matters, deal in the provision of weapons, and write letters which rise far above practical necessity to illustrate a strong sense of her character. Lady Brilliana Harley should not be underestimated, and neither should her letters.

Tryfan and the Ogwen Valley
by Colin See-Paynton

CHRIS HALL

no ifs

i am a man more
sinnin than cinder genst
having emerjd
out v th great no where
uttering onli
screechen catterwaul
                    from th outset
                        dreaming alone
                            nd given t ructions
                              whyforwayfare
ever th tendenci
                t th magnetic poles

it was however
yonder by th lichgate
that th first hints v th heathen
gave way t th hymns v th heretic
nd those fierce visions
(yes i said visions)
v a prophesied
              here nd now

nd when they said
it was
      time t wake up
shaking th cradl nd smashing th skylight
i held clenchtight
t th tenets v th dreamstate
nd th imperativs v nightmare

t this day
there cannot be
even th slightest
                trace v regret

nor spurious soothsaying
no ands
no buts
amendments
codicils
th one truth being
beyond all others
there are no ifs in histori

this then was
th starting point
th setting out
shorn v manifesto nd v balderdash
unlaydnd nd unburdend
by th encumbrences v ancestri
blind tradition
tyranni v
a semblant inheritance

so when y ask me
how come
i sit here in th windoseat
cracking th heads from shellfish
n pretending t be
part v th graffiti
th reply
tho not necessarily elydid
purposefulli obscurantist
will still be
in need v deconstruction
discernment

some measure
v disentangling

d maybe
(yes i said just maybe)
i might have answerd
that they came looking
f a younger man
full v hope

springsong
a measure v empathi
iskra
that spark

nd yet
(yes yet)
it can still be promulgated
that in this dreamin city
those fine
(so fine)
buttresses fly
against them surjinspires

nd i espy
down there by th riverbank
that old bridge
clings on regardless
v wagonloads
vagabonds
th muleteers

nd in th end
(if end there be)
let it be said
there was onli
one passage possibl
nd that would always be
th one that was taken

now
when night comes
i will myself surmise
was it here?
or there?
or someplace in th great wherever
that which was lost
can be now be retrievd
gatherd

comprehendid?

nd will
even i   sinbad th sinnaman

as a last resort

look up t th vast expanse v th highest v all th heavens
nd th lowest depths v th deepest v all th hells

nd breathe that one word

kismet?

TOM GOUTHWAITE

Cedar

Shadows high
along the gables,
wide and cool
across a level lawn;

fragrance,
a whisper of needles
lazing the sound
of afternoon.

Touch the bark,
feel the synapse
of an era,

the impulse
down your fingers
of a loss,

a limbic spark
of Solomon's
Jerusalem.

THOR BACON

Robert Capa's Leica

Which is worse – to go like Gerda Taro,
war photographer, torso crushed by a tank;
or to bleed-out twenty years later murmuring her name?

The mind goes on plinking those two notes
while the heart's symphony spins and swells.
We're still upset that Fred and Ginger never married.

I'll warn you in the conquerors' tongue: beware
their dirge of paper-clips, the algorithms
they postulate for love, that albino crow.

Hunching in bunkers they right-click, counting down the shift.
On the news a child rolls pita bread with a mortar casing.
Everyone is tweeting *which side are you on*.

You're right to call my bluff – I'm just a pianist
who never learnt to play. Capa dove with the G.I.s
and cocked his camera made in Germany.

The curlew reels with her slender beak;
the wind strokes the salty gorse. At Omaha Beach
I'm told the waves still make that hushing sound.

OLIVER COMINS

Sunflowers at Night

Across this field, a whole crop of sunflowers
is stepping down from duty. With no light left
to tap a genetic compulsion, they use free will.

All those hours spent staring up are finished.
Some turn to face their weary companions,
yellow crests illuminating after-shift colloquy.

Others bow bright petal-sets where they stand,
guarding their privacy. Alone among so many,
they attempt to retrieve a little of themselves.

Soon, a full moon will rise and appear to shine
above them. She is sun's slave too, observing
their twilight discourse, heads heavy with seed.

OLIVER MORT

Boat in Belfast

Behind the Co-op and Dominos
on the Antrim Road
a boat is marooned
among a row of terraced houses.

Every day I wander down to the bakery
to get my lunch I see it. The same
big bastard rat runs around it
as if it's Noah's Ark.

The rain does fall. Every day there's a flood
of drizzle. Heaven's half-hearted
attempt at participation to wash away
the bookmakers' receipts, the dog poo,
the pizza boxes left on the street.
I'm always soaked. That boat never floats.

KAY SYRAD

Chagall, window

There's a red horse in the centre –
red for happiness once, when it was,
arcs of red at the top of the arch
and the great wave of blue-above-

blue in the lower half, curving up
to a higher blue and the mystery
of suffering, blue purpose of it
(Christ's slight chest is yellow lift)

dash of white light here at the edge,
all the blue and yellow and red
(love) and four or five times green,
the smallest green

                                        and nothing,
nothing can prepare you for this.

MIRIAM CRAIG

Sunset

I watched each flat wave
smooth its hand along the shore

and tried to shake loose a pebble
from the sandal of thought

until, giving up, I turned
to see the sunset weighing down

breathing red life into the sand,
the sea, my skin, doing what a sunset does –

clasping its burning arms
round everything, to draw me into one

bright, hammered foil of air and land.
I wanted to stay until the end.

Back at the house, my friends were waiting.
What if the earth had failed

to turn its shoulder to the sun,
like someone propped against the sofa arm

when a film begins, intending
every moment till the credits, to get up?

HUBERT MOORE

At the feeding-station

In your last long far too scarce
summer days you knew this scene
without looking: the darting
of bird after bird from the hedge
to where the peanuts hang,
the nyjer, the sunflower seed.

The map of it, bird-lanes
flitting out to the feeding-station
and back, you must have known by
heart, your struggling delightable heart.

Thought-lanes follow bird-lanes, dart
to wherever you went when you died
and back, beaks loaded,
woodpecker, blue tit, sparrow
and your beloved family
starting again on their lives.

I still don't know
if the dead come flitting back
to feed on the lives of the living.

The living though, the left-alive
grieving ones, they're rich
in thought-lanes, story-lanes, voice-lanes.
They flit from the hedge to feed on you.

ROSIE JACKSON

An Anchorite Laments the Destruction of Her Cell, 1537

I laid down my life, so He could make wine out of me,
jug after jug. I wanted to be trodden by His feet.

But the Lord God has taken a battering ram to the heavens.
He has broken the night into pieces & days are too bright,

stars too sharp, prayers too feeble to be heard over such
great distances. Is this what it is to be scorched by the fires

of Love? Has devotion become so alien in this world,
it must be dismantled, stone by stone? I pick over the ruins

as if there's been an earthquake – a solitary, a woman who rattles
like a tinker with her pans, yet nothing to sell or mend. Oh, return me

to the discipline of the squint, the blind comfort of darkness.
Give me back the cover of His wings, my white apron of chastity.

I wasn't meant to be resurrected. My vow was unto death. This is how
Lazarus must have felt – nervous of each noise & open space, raped by sunlight.

Magnetic Power in Henry Vaughan's Poetry[1]

MAI MATSUMOTO

That magnetism played a significant role in Henry Vaughan's poetry has already been noted. A. U. Chapman has shown that it was an evolving image, changing over time from the early love poetry to become something quite different in later poems in *Silex Scintillans*.[2] According to Chapman, in earlier poems such as *Poems with the Tenth Satire of Juvenal Englished* (1646), his use of magnetism is 'characterized to some extent by "wit" or learning'.[3] The expressions related to magnetism there are frequently mere figures of speech, involving banal metaphors such as that of the attraction of the beloved lady compared to the power of a magnet. By the time he wrote '*To his Learned Friend and Loyal Fellow-Prisoner*, Thomas Powel *of* Cant. Doctor of Divinity', one of his epistolary poems, Vaughan had clearly read the magnetic philosophy of William Gilbert's *De Magnete* (1600), one of whose discoveries was that 'in magnetism, motion is not caused by attraction but by a coming together or agreeing together of both parts'.[4] Chapman, then, argues that Vaughan used this idea in the poem to emphasize that 'friendship is not a one-sided matter but requires that both parties are "animate"'.[5] It is only after this poem that 'Vaughan feels free to use magnetic imagery in any but purely metaphorical ways'.[6]

Alan Rudrum expanded Chapman's reading of magnetism beyond the mere concept or words, 'magnet' and 'magnetic', and saw it more as part of Vaughan's spiritual cosmology, deeply indebted to his brother's Hermetic Philosophy. While

---

1 This article is a slightly revised version of a paper presented at the 23rd Colloquium of The Vaughan Association. I am grateful to Professor Takashi Yoshinaka, Dr. Joseph Sterrett and anonymous readers for valuable suggestions to improve this paper.

2 A. U. Chapman, 'Vaughan and Magnetic Philosophy', *Southern Review* 4 (1970-1971), pp. 215-226. Alan Rudrum, 'An Aspect of Vaughan's Hermeticism: The Doctrine of Cosmic Sympathy', *Studies in English Literature, 1500-1900, Vol. 14* (1974), pp. 129-138.

3 Chapman, p. 216.

4 Chapman, p. 226, note 25.

5 Chapman, p. 221.

6 Chapman, p. 222.

one of the purposes of Chapman's article is to question the degree of influence of hermeticism on Vaughan's views; Rudrum, on the contrary, argues for its significance in Vaughan's work. Rudrum classified Vaughan's magnetic images in 'the mature poems' into three categories. The first is the '"commerce" kept between God and his creatures'; the second is 'the influence of macrocosm on microcosm' (an influence which the Renaissance hermeticists thought of as operable in reverse); and the third is 'an influence operating through the senses'.[7] From the larger perspective of Vaughan's poetic career, roughly involving a movement from the secular to the religious, however, Rudrum's categories may be reordered and rephrased as follows: Vaughan's poetic magnetism operating in the lower sphere of the universe, such magnetism operating between the lower and the upper spheres, and then, the magnetism between human souls and God.

As for the last category, critics and readers have noted that the idea of faith in seventeenth-century poetry can be explained by the operation of magnetism in a certain sense. For example, God was frequently described as a loadstone which lifted up the soul of man. In this paper, however, by refering to the thought of Jacob Boehme, I would like to argue that Vaughan implies the operation of magnetic power in a wider range of his religious beliefs, such as when he describes the resurrection of the body.

When we consider Vaughan's expressions related to magnetism in the context of religious thought, it is necessary that we take into account the circumstances of the 1640s and 1650s. It seems that the former topic and the latter issue, however, have been discussed separately. For instance, on the one hand, A. U. Chapman has suggested that in Vaughan's religious verse the poet sees 'magnetic imagery as a suitable substitute for light imagery'.[8] Peter Thomas, on the other hand, has argued that the term 'the new lights' in Vaughan's poems alludes to the puritan sectarians who were making inroads into Wales during the 1650s.[9] Since the advent of New Historicism, Vaughan's words and images have been fruitfully re-considered in their political and historical contexts, but, oddly enough, Vaughan's magnetism has not yet been interpreted politically. Neither Chapman nor Rudrum place magnetic theory in any political context. Thus, I would like to re-consider Vaughan's expressions involving magnetism in their contemporary religio-political context. First, however, let us begin by synthesizing Chapman's and Rudrum's findings in order to suggest that Vaughan's use of the concept of magnetism is not necessarily divided between the secular and the religious poetry.

7 Rudrum, p. 133.

8 Chapman, p. 233.

9 Peter Thomas, 'The Language of Light: Henry Vaughan and the Puritans', *Scintilla 3*, (1999), pp. 9-29.

I. Magnetism that Operates Between Human Beings

In one of the early 'Amoret' poems, Vaughan likens 'true love' to the force of a magnetic field:

> Thus to the North the Loadstones move,
> And thus to them th'enamour'd steel aspires:
> Thus, *Amoret*,
> I doe affect[.]
> (Henry Vaughan, '*To* Amoret, *of the difference 'twixt him, and other Lovers,* and what true *Love* is', ll. 29-32)[10]

In spite of the speaker's desire to differentiate his passionate love, his expression is not very different from the common lovers' complaint in traditional sonnets. In Vaughan's other love poems, 'sympathy' and 'influence', the words employed in Platonism, are virtually synonymous with magnetic force.[11] For example, in 'To Amoret, Walking in a Starry Evening', the speaker calls to his beloved as follows:

> But, *Amoret*, such is my fate,
> That if thy face a Starre,
> Had shin'd from farre,
> I am perswaded in that state
> 'Twixt thee, and me,
> Of some predestin'd sympathie.
> (Henry Vaughan, 'To Amoret, Walking in a Starry EVENING', ll. 13-18)

Here, by 'sympathie', Vaughan means 'A (real or supposed) affinity between certain things, by virtue of which they are similarly or correspondingly affected by the same influence, affect or influence one another, or attract or tend towards each other' (*OED*, 1). And in another of the Amoret poems, Vaughan uses the word 'influence' in a similar way:

> If Creatures then that have no sense,
> But the loose tye of influence,
> ....

10 Donald R. Dickson, Alan Rudrum, Robert Wilcher. ed. *The Works of Henry Vaughan: Introduction and Texts 1646-1652* (Oxford: Clarendon Press, 2018), p. 22. Hereafter, Vaughan's works will be cited in the text from this edition.

11 See Rudrum, pp. 130-131, Chapman, pp. 216-217.

At such vast distance can agree,
  Why *Amoret*, why should not wee.
    (Henry Vaughan, 'To Amoret GONE FROM HIM', ll. 19-20, 22-23)

The important thing for our concern is that Vaughan thinks creatures including stones and magnets have 'influence', even if they have *no* life. However, Vaughan's concept of 'influence' changes in the poems published after 1650.[12]

In the poem entitled, '*To his Learned Friend and Loyal Fellow-Prisoner*, Thomas Powel *of* Cant. Doctor of Divinity', Vaughan challenges the idea that materials without life can have spiritual commerce:

    'Tis a kind Soul in *Magnets*, that attones
Such two hard things as *Iron* are and *Stones*,
And in their dumb *compliance* we learn more
Of Love, than ever Books could speak before.
For though <u>*attraction*</u> hath got all the name,
As if that *power* but from one side came,
Which both unites; yet, where there is no *sence*,
There is no *Passion*, nor *Intelligence*:
And so by consequence we cannot state
A Commerce, unless both we animate.
For senseless things, . . .
Are deaf, and feel no Invitation;
. . .
    'Tis then no *Heresie* to end the strife
With such rare Doctrine as gives *Iron* life.
    (Henry Vaughan, '*To his Learned Friend and Loyal Fellow-Prisoner*,
        Thomas Powel *of* Cant. Doctor of Divinity', ll. 7-18, 21-22)

What is noteworthy is that the magnetic force Vaughan describes here does work in two directionals. As Chapman and Rudrum have already argued, the poet uses the theory which William Gilbert expounded in his *De Magnete*.[13] According to Gilbert, Magnetic power is defined not as an 'attraction', i.e., 'magnetic attraction: the action of a magnet or loadstone in drawing and attaching iron to itself' (*OED*, 5. B.), but as the power of uniting two things with each other. It is termed, 'coition', which is the action of 'Going or coming to-

12 See Rudrum, pp. 132-133, Chapman, pp. 220-221.

13 See Chapman, pp. 218-219.

gether; meeting; uniting' (*OED* 1) or 'A mutual tendency of bodies toward one another, as of the iron and loadstone' (*OED* 1 b). Another important aspect of Vaughan's use of the theory of Gilbert is that both materials involved in this 'coition' should have life, whether they are stones or human souls. Gilbert's well-known contribution to the study of magnetism as a scientific field is that he maintains that the Earth itself is a great loadstone.[14] This theory contradicted the belief that the compass points towards the North because the polar star has a magnetic power. Gilbert's new theory is deeply bound up with his animistic world view, in which he maintained ardently that all creatures including stones have their own life. The reason why some rational and materialist scientists such as Francis Bacon objected to this magnetic theory is that it seemed to them too mysterious or even too superstitious. However, during the first half of the seventeenth century, Gilbert's idea was supported by Sir Thomas Browne, Rober Fludd and others. William Barlow, for example, following Gilbert's theory of magnetism, in his *Magneticall Aduertisements*, states that the magnet works in two directions and both objects in the magnetic field have their own sensation:

> The *Attraction* (commonly so called) of the *Loadstone* is rightly to be termed, *Concursion, Confluence,* or *Coition,* because it is the running or vigorous meeting together of two *Magneticall* bodies hauing a mutuall inclination the one to ioyne with the other, or by any other name, bearing like sense.[15]

Given the 'rare doctrine', which Vaughan seems to espouse in 'To his Learned Friend and Loyal Fellow-Prisoner, Thomas Powel of Cant. Doctor of Divinity', we can infer that Vaughan's magnetic theory relates to the theological idea of death and resurrection. When Vaughan says that on the last day of the world, God's 'Effectual informing influence' (l. 28) 'shall be shed / By the great Lord of Life into the Dead' (ll. 19-20), he implies that the parts of dead bodies, what John Donne called 'scattered bodies' ('At the round earth's imagined corners', l. 4), will be gathered together and united with their souls again, because they are animated at Doomsday and become magnetic.[16]

The idea that magnetic material should have its own life is consistent with Vaughan's persistent belief that creatures including stones must have 'sense'

14 Chapman, p. 219

15 William Barlow, *Magneticall Aduertisements: or Diuers Pertinent Obseruations, and Approued Experiments* (1618), pp. 2-3.

16 John Donne, *The Complete Poems of John Donne*, ed. Robin Robins (Longman, 2008), p. 535.

beyond 'the loose tye of influence'. In the poem which begins with the line 'And do they so?', Vaughan's belief that every creature must have life seems to be more strongly embraced and the poet denies in the form of rhetorical questions the thought expressed in the imagery of his earlier love poems. Vaughan thus rejects the view of nature which was widely accepted in the seventeenth century:

> And do they so? have they a Sense
> Of ought but Influence?
> Can they their heads lift, and expect,
> And grone too? Why th'Elect
> Can do no more: my volume sed
> They were all dull, and dead,
> They judg'd them senselesse, and their state
> Wholly Inanimate.
> Go, go; Seal up thy looks,
> And burn thy books.
>
> (Henry Vaughan, 'And do they so?', ll. 1-10)

Presumably, Vaughan refers to books expressing some form of materialism and criticizes the idea of creatures as 'all dull, and dead'. Thomas Vaughan agreed with his twin brother, also stating that all creatures have an ability to have commerce with each other, because every creature has the same spiritual essence:

> The normal, celestial, ethereal part of man is that whereby we do move, see, feel, taste and smell, and have a commerce with all material objects whatsoever. It is the same in us as in beasts, and it is derived from heaven [. . .] to all the inferior earthly creatures.[17]

The 'commerce' which Thomas Vaughan mentions here is partly, but not entirely, explained by the vertical force which the seventeenth century believed worked upon creatures on earth from heaven.

17 Thomas Vaughan, *Anthroposophia Theomagica, or, A Discourse of the Nature of Man and His State After Death* (London, 1656), p. 38. Thomas also finds the spirit in minerals. He says, 'Spirit is in Man, in Beasts, in Vegetables, in Minerals; and in every thing it is the *meditate* Cause of Composition and Multiplication. [. . .] I affirm this spirit to be in Minerals' (*ibid.*, p. 39).

II. The Commerce between Macrocosm and Microcosm and Magnetic Power

Many people in the seventeenth-century believed in the power of astrological influence, the effect of the stars on creatures. For example, Thomas Vaughan explained:

> Man is made subject to the Influence of Stars, and is partly dispos'd of by the Coelestial harmony.[18]

The idiosyncratic point of view about nature, perhaps peculiar to Thomas and Henry Vaughan, is that the 'influence' from heaven works not only upon man but also upon every creature on earth. Thomas also sees the power of 'influence' in growing plants:

> There is not an Herb here *below*, but he hath a *star* in *Heaven above*, and the *star* strikes him with her *Beam* and says to him, *Grow*.[19]

It seems that this hermetic idea of Thomas led Henry to describe herbs as watching for the star. The downward effect, as Thomas asserts, which works upon plants from the stars of heaven, is reversed and described as the upward gaze of plants to the stars in Henry's poem, 'The Favour':

> Some kinde herbs here, though low & far,
> Watch for, and know their loving star.
>
> (Henry Vaughan, 'The Favour', ll. 7-8)

The poem entitled 'The Starre' is typical in showing a two-way exchange between heaven and earth, a sympathetic and magnetic relationship between the star and the beautiful object or creature on earth:

> What ever 'tis, whose beauty here below
> Attracts thee thus & makes thee stream & flow,
> And wind and curle, and wink and smile,
> Shifting thy gate and guile:
>
> Though thy close commerce nought at all imbarrs
> My present search[.]
>
> (Henry Vaughan, 'The Starre', ll. 1-6)

18 *Ibid.*, p. 39.

19 Thomas Vaughan, *Lumen de Lumine, or A new Magicall Light* (London, 1651), p. 88.

As the title suggests, the poem is a meditation upon a star and the opening stanza illustrates Vaughan's concept of magnetism. Here, the poet asserts that the light of the star is attracted by the beauty on earth. The reason why magnetism works here is that heaven and earth have the same essence; at least partly, they are homogeneous. According to Thomas Vaughan,

> Heaven it self was originally extracted from Inferiors, yet not so intirely [=entirely],but some portion of the Heavenly Natures remained still below, and are the very same essence and substance with the separated stars and skies.[20]

Henry Vaughan also recognizes this commerce between the stars and creatures on earth as effected by a kind of magnetic power:

> These are the Magnets which so strongly move
> And work all night upon thy light and love,
> As beauteous shapes, we know not why,
> Command and guide the eye.
> (Henry Vaughan, 'The Starre', ll. 21-24)

Thomas's and Henry's thoughts can be explicated in terms of the ideas of the German mystic, Jacob Boehme. He believed that plants remember the joyfulness they used to enjoy in their heavenly state before the Fall, because the 'Archaeus', the enegetic power in Heaven, still remains in them, and they desire to go back to that Heavenly place:

> [. . .] the Earth, [. . .] is so very hungry after the [influence and vertue of the] Starres, and the *Spiritus Mundi*, (viz. after the Spirit from whence it proceeded in the beginning) that it hath no Rest, for hunger [. . .] we see in this hunger [. . .] how the undermost *Archæus* of the Earth attracteth the uttermost subtile *Archæus* from the Constellations above the Earth: where this compacted ground from the uppermost *Archæus*, longeth for its ground againe and putteth it selfe forth towards the uppermost; in which putting forth, the growing of Metals, Plants and Trees, hath its Originall. For, the *Archæus* of the Earth becommeth

20 Thomas Vaughan, *Magia Adamica : or The Antiquity of Magic, and the Descent Thereof from Adam Downwards, proved. Whereunto is Added a Perfect, and Full Discoverie of the True Coelum Terrae, or the Magician's Heavenly Chaos, and First Matter of All Things* (London, 1651), p. 68.

> thereby exceeding joyfull, because it tasteth and feeleth its first ground in it selfe againe: and in this Joy all things spring out of the Earth[.][21]

What Boehme calls *Archæus* generates magnetic power between heaven and earth. The 'uttermost subtile *Archæus*' works upon the 'undermost *Archæus*' on earth.

Alternatively, the relationship between heaven and earth can be explained by the theory of correspondence. Thomas Vaughan, referring to 'Anima Mundi',[22] i.e., the world soul, describes the magnetic commerce kept between heaven and earth in Platonic terms:

> [. . .] the *Universal Magnet,* which binds this *great Frame,* and moves all the *Members* of it to a *Mutuall Compassion.*[23]

In other words, the 'universal magnet' works in the world soul. In addition, Thomas finds the mutual force of magnetism in the vertical vector of universal correspondence.

> . . . the infallible *Magnet*, the Mystery of Union. By this all Things may be attracted whether Physicall, or Metaphysicall, be the distance never so great. This is *Jacobs Ladder*: without this there is no Ascent, or Descent either Influentiall, or Personall.[24]

Thomas describes 'the infallible Magnet' which unites all things to the world soul. In this context, the biblical story of 'Jacobs Ladder' is also explained by the magnetic power. Thomas maintains that both ascent and descent on the ladder are made possible by the operation of magnetism.

The rise and the fall explained by the magnetic power connecting heaven and earth can also be found in Henry Vaughan's poems. The bi-directional movements, both the rise from earth to heaven, and the fall from heaven to earth, are detectable in the poem entitled 'Midnight'.

> I doe survey
> Each busie Ray [of the Stars]
> And how they work, and wind,
> And wish each beame
> My soul doth streame,
> With the like ardour shin'd[.]
>
> (Henry Vaughan, 'Midnight', ll. 5-10)

21 Jacob Boehme, *The Clavis or Key* (London, 1647), pp. 23-24.
22 Thomas Vaughan, *Anthroposophia Theomagica*, p. 38.
23 Thomas Vaughan, *Magia Adamica*, p. 80.
24 Thomas Vaughan, *Anthroposophia Theomagica*, p. 23.

Here, there is a contrast between the 'ardour' of the stars and Vaughan's own lack of ardour: it is his 'wish' that the beams streaming from his soul could shine with the same ardour as that of the stars. This means that he desires 'each beam' of the stars to influence 'My soul' so it may awaken the same 'ardour'. Given the mutual force of 'attraction' between heaven and earth, however, it is 'My soul' that could make each ray of the stars 'streame'. The poet's soul 'here below', as we saw in 'The Starre', could attract the star and makes it 'stream and flow' (ll. 1, 2). Thus, it may be said that the subject and the object in this sentence are interchangeable; in other words, we can read these lines in two ways: the poet wishes that 'each beam streams my soul', and that 'my soul streams each beam'. It may also be argued that this ambiguity in the syntax indicates the bi-directional relation between the stars and the soul,[25] and at least the poet's prayer that the grace of God and the man's devotion should work upon each other.

Interestingly, Vaughan says that the stars shine with their 'ardour'. By implication, he exhorts the reader to show his or her 'ardour'. The fact that Vaughan did not use the word 'zeal' may be important, because it was a politically charged word by which Puritans described their faith. As Philip West has argued, using the word 'zeal' elsewhere, Vaughan condemns their fanaticism.[26] For example, in the poem 'The Constellation', Vaughan insists that there would be 'peace still, and no war' (l. 32) on earth as well as in heaven, if earth corresponded to heaven. However, the noise of those who are 'crying zeale' (l. 40) breaks the connection between heaven and earth. In this poem, too, as in 'Midnight', the stars and human souls do not make their 'coition' possible, to the poet's regret. It may be said that, in Vaughan's poems, ideally, true faith is represented as a mutually attractive magnetic power, which draws celestial things and men's souls together. In the poem 'The Starre', Vaughan says that 'God a Commerce states, and sheds / His Secret on their heads' (ll. 27-28). Many of us, however, have lost the innate magnet in our souls. As a consequence, Puritan 'zeal' represents a kind of false faith.

In the next section, I shall focus on magnetism between man and God, what may be called magnetic theology.

25 See Takashi Yoshinaka, *The Poems of Henry Vaughan.* (Japanese Translation) (Hiroshima: U of Hiroshima P, 2006), p. 101. Another example of the interchangeability of the subject and the object in Vaughan's syntax, which reflects his idea of the commerce kept 'between the visible temporal universe and its eternal counterpart in the mind of God' (Rudrum, p. 133), can be found in 'The Night' : 'his own living works did my Lord hold / And lodge alone' ('The Night', ll. 21-22). See also Yoshinaka, p. 382.

26 Phillip West, *Henry Vaughan's Silex Scintillans: Scripture Uses* (Oxford: OUP, 2001), pp. 147-180.

III. God and Magnetism

John Donne, in one of his *Holy Sonnets*, likens the way in which God draws men towards Him to magnetic attraction. Typically, the iron represents the poet's human heart:

> Thy grace may wing me to prevent his [= our old subtle foe's] art,
> And thou like ad'mant draw mine iron heart.
>
> (John Donne, 'Thou hast made me', ll. 13-14)

The word 'adamant' is 'Identified with the loadstone or magnet' (*OED* †3. a.). Thanks to the 'grace' of God, the speaker can ascend to heaven. Donne emphasizes that this ascension is possible because God 'wings' men, in other words, because God draws men towards Him by His divine magnetic power. Here, the means of ascension, whether 'wing' or 'magnet', is not specified clearly, but the vector of magnetic force is in one direction; that is, Donne is invoking the theory of magnetism that prevailed before Gilbert's discovery of mutual attraction. Likewise, in De Montenay's emblem book, the image of the magnet is used as a starting point for contemplating the merciful, but absolute power of Christ:

> Leike aſ the Magnet that Iron thuſ,
> Draw to him, and never refuſ;
> So thuſ Creiſt, aur ſauier deare,
> Al ſuch, which him truly fier;
> And brings them, to hiſ Father ſweet,
> Wher all the angelſ they ſhall meet;
> For non but he, kan vſin to that pleaſ,
> Help: Aut of their miſery and diſtreſſe[.][27]

27 De Montenay, *A Booke of Armes, or Remembrance* (London, 1619), p. 52.

The corresponding motto reads: 'The iron is attracted by a magnetic power, we are drawn to Christ by the merciful God'. In the context of alchemy, Christ was often compared to the quintessence or Philosopher's Stone, which, in turn, was believed to contain an important substance called magnesia. [28] This may be a further reason why Vaughan's theological use of magnetism was not merely a figurative one. He, with his alchemist brother, may have been convinced by the idea of Christ as a magnet.

The image of God exercising power over man's heart recalls the Emblem attached to *Silex Sintillans* published in 1650.

As Rudrum, Dickson and other scholars have suggested, the stone in the emblem represents the heart of the sinful poet.[29] Rudrum translates Vaughan's Latin poem into English as follows:

> More divine breath hath entreated me with its gentle action and admonished me in vain with holy murmur. I was a flint – dead and silent. [. . .] You allow for my reformation by another means, and alter your approach. You draw nearer and break that mass which is my rocky heart, and that which was formerly stone is now made flesh.[30]

28 See Mai Matsumoto, *Henry Vaughan and the Philosopher's Stone* (Japanese) (Tokyo: Kinseido, 2016), pp. 91-95. See also Theophrastus Paracelsus, *Paracelsus his Aurora & Treasure of the Philosophers . . . Faithfully Englished And published by W.D* (London, 1659), pp. 1-2, 149-150, Jacob Boehme, *Signatura Rerum* (London, 1651), sig. A4.

29 See D. R. Dickson, *The Fountain of Living Waters: The Typology of the Waters of Life in Herbert, Vaughan, and Traherne* (Colombia: U of Missouri P, 1987), pp. 124-129, Louis L. Martz, *The Paradise Within* (New Heaven: Yale UP, 1964), p. 5. See also J. D. Simmonds, *Masques of God* (Pittsburgh: U of Pittsburgh, 1972), p. 153, Thomas O. Calhoun, *Henry Vaughan, the Achievement of Silex Scintillans* (New Jersey: Associated U P, 1981), p. 138.

30 Henry Vaughan, *The Complete Poems*, ed. Alan Rudrum (Harmondsworth: Penguin, 1977), p. 137.

Vaughan says that God came nearer and broke the poet's rocky, stubborn heart. As with the grace of the Calvinistic God in Donne's Holy Sonnet, the poet attaches a great importance to God's power. But, considering that Gilbert's theory that magnetic force works in both directions had already spread by the mid seventeenth century, we may assume that Vaughan regarded the poet's heart as a stone loaded with at least a latent magnetic force. To the best of my knowledge, no one has pointed out the fact that Vaughan's heart in the emblem is uplifted in the air. That is to say, unlike the heart in De Money's emblem, which is 'attracted by a magnetic poer', Vaughan's stony heart rises because it is enlivened, that is, its life and magnetic force are restored by God.

Poets frequently say that the soul needs wings when she goes up to Heaven. So, when William Habington looks over 'the bright / Coelestial sphere', his 'soul her wings doth spread / And heaven-ward flies'. (William Habington, 'Nox Nocti Indicat Scientiam David.', ll. 1-2, 5-6).[31] Vaughan himself in '*The importunate Fortune, written to Doctor Powel of* Cantare' encourages his soul to get up, saying 'thy fire / Is now refin'd & nothing left to tire, / Or clog thy wings'. Writers who took the position of Arminianism thought that men would need good works for salvation. Therefore, as Yoshinaka has noted, using the image of the 'wing' implies that men could rise to heaven partly by their own force, not only by God's grace, stressing a mutuality like that in Gilbert's theory of magnetism.[32]

Sometimes, however, Vaughan describes men's ascension to heaven as not involving the use of any wing:

Hee [= Christ] alone
And none else can
Bring bone to bone
And rebuild man,
And by his all subduing might
Make clay ascend more quick than light.

(Henry Vaughan, 'Ascension-Hymn', ll. 37-42)

As we saw in the first section, the lines from '*To his Learned Friend and Loyal Fellow-Prisoner*, Thomas Powel *of* Cant. Doctor of Divinity' suggest that Vaughan thinks the divine power of resurrection, which 'bring[s] bone to bone' here, is tantamount to magnetic power. According to A. J. Penny, Jacob Boehme

31 William Habington, *Castara* (London, 1640), p. 192.

32 See Yoshinaka, p. 225.

intimates that 'at the time of the general resurrection [. . .] the law of spiritual affinity will then be irresistible and every magnet will draw its own natural adherents'. Based on Boehme's statement that 'The magnetical attraction is the beginning of nature', Penny claims that 'the same creative law will rule when to the spiritual body a body in ultimates is restored'.[33] If we can assume, here in Vaughan's 'Ascension-Hymn', that the power of resurrection is identical to that of ascension, Christ's 'all subduing might' which enables man to soar up to Heaven (or which, in other poems, sprouts, and flies with, 'wings') may mean the operation of a divine magnetic force. If so, Vaughan's magnetic ascension implies true faith on the part of the human soul.

Vaughan thinks that man originally had a magnet in his soul and knew the way to heaven. Man, however, lost his way in religious corruption and, in contemporary terms, in the turmoil of the Civil War. In the poem entitled 'Man', Vaughan says that man has fallen into the state in which he keeps knocking at all the doors:

> Man hath stil either toyes, or Care,
> He hath no root, nor to one place is ty'd
> But ever restless and Irregular
> About this Earth doth run and ride,
> He knows he hath a home, but scarce knows where[.]
> ....
> He knocks at all doors, strays and roams,
> Nay hath not so much <u>wit as some stones have</u>
> Which in the darkest nights point to their homes,
> By some hid sense their Maker gave[.]
>
> (Henry Vaughan, 'Man', ll. 15-19, 22-25)

As Rudrum has noted, the 'stones' here are 'loadstones' or magnets.[34] The way 'to their homes' is both vertical and horizontal: the expression implies not only that Man has to rise up to his heavenly home but also that man has to sail the ocean of life safely back to the port. Compare Hugo's *Pia Desideria* (1624), one of the emblems which depicts the needle of a compass pointing to the North:.

33 A.J. Penny, *Studies in Jacob Bohme* (Wipf & Stock, 2016), p. 456. See also Jacob Bohme, *Concerning the Election of Grace, or Of Gods Will towards Man* (London, 1623), p. 11.

34 Henry Vaughan, *The Complete Poems,* ed. Alan Rudrum (Harmondsworth: Penguin, 1977), p. 586, See also *The Works of Henry Vaughan* (Oxford: Clarendon Press, 2018), p. 975.

So, by ſtrange sympathy, the faithful *Steel*
Does the lov'd *Pole*'s magnetick infl'ence feel,
By whoſe kind conduct the ſafe *Pylot* ſteers
A ſteddy courſe, till the wiſh'd Port appears.
......
Like theſe, Almighty Love, to Thee I flie[.][35]

In likening God's divine power compared to the 'magnetick infl'ence', Hugo espouses the pre-Gilbertian theory that the North Pole has a magnetic force. The 'Pylot steers' his ship by the loadstar as a loadstone and safely comes back to the port as his home.

In the poem entitled 'The Tempest', Vaughan describes how the creatures try to rise 'upwards' and point out to man 'the way home':

All things here shew him heaven; *Waters* that fall
    Chide, and fly up; *Mists* of corruptest fome
    Quit their first beds & mount; trees, herbs, flowres, all
Strive upwards stil, and point him the way home.
(Henry Vaughan, 'The Tempest', ll. 25-28)

In addition, Vaughan describes all creatures moving upward to heaven, using a musical term, 'key':

35 Herman Hugo, *Pia Desideria*. Englished by Edm. Arwaker (1686), p. 193.

> All have their *keyes*, and set *ascents*; but man
> Though he knows these, and hath more of his own,
> Sleeps at the ladders foot[.]
> (Henry Vaughan, 'The Tempest', ll. 37-39)

What should be emphasized is that all creatures except man have their own keys, just as Vaughan describes the situation of human beings in 'Man'. Here, the poet stresses man's idleness. He is sleeping at the foot of the 'ladder'. As we saw earlier, Thomas Vaughan illustrates the movements of ascent and descent on Jacob's ladder as a manifestation of the magnetic force. In this context, the sleeping man at the foot of the ladder signifies that he has lost his own magnetic power. On the other hand, all other creatures descend or ascend in their keys by a magnetic ladder, and thanks to this motion, they keep their holiness.

In Vaughan's poems, especially in *Silex Scintillans*, all creatures except man are frequently described as if they harness their magnetic power to maintain their commerce with God. In the poem which begins with the line 'Sure, there's a tye of bodies!', the built-in magnet of the creatures is attracted to light:

> Absents within the Line Conspire, and *Sense*
> Things distant doth unite,
> Herbs sleep unto the *East*, and some fowles thence
> Watch the Returns of light[.]
> (Henry Vaughan, 'Sure, there's a tye of bodies!', ll. 9-12)

Here, the magnetic force that unites is synonymous with 'Sense', and the magnetic field between the creatures is described as the 'Line'. The image of birds magnetically drawn to light leads into the final section, in which Vaughan exploits it for political purposes.

IV. Magnetism and Light

First, we should recall Chapman's remark that 'Vaughan seems to see magnetic imagery as a suitable substitute for light imagery when he wishes to express the idea of a commerce between God and His creatures continuing during the darkness of night'.[36] A typical example can be found in 'Cock-crowing' which begins:

36 Chapman, p. 233.

Father of lights! what Sunnie seed,
What glance of day hast thou confin'd
Into this bird? To all the breed
This busie Ray thou hast assign'd;
Their magnetisme works all night,
And dreams of Paradise and light.

Their eyes watch for the mourning-hue,
Their little grain expelling night
So shines and sings as if it knew
The path unto the house of light.

(Henry Vaughan, 'Cock-crowing', ll. 1-10)

The phrase 'Father of Lights!' is derived from James 1:17 in the Bible: 'Every good gist and every effect is from above, and cometh down from the Father of light'. As Pettet notes, this expression is also used by Thomas Vaughan.[37] What should be emphasized is that Vaughan, talking about the relationship between God and his creatures, superimposes the imagery of light on that of magnetism. The cock has a kind of magnetic light and this power expels the darkness of the night.

In the seventeenth century, Vaughan was not the only person who recognized that the power of magnetism was similar to that of light. For example, Robert Fluddsays:

> The Iron therefore like a vivified mass, meeting with the Load-stone, doth easily emit his beams of love unto the Load-stone, who doth as greedily suck or draw them, by means of his inward earthly Martial Spirits, even unto her Center, and by the attraction of the Iron's formal beams, draweth with it all the Iron body.[38]

And it may be worth noting that Athanasius Kircher devised a sunflower clock by employing what he regarded as the magnetic power of light, which is what we now call 'photonasty'. In his *Magnes, sive De Arte Magnetica* (1641), he believed that the Sun itself was a magnet and that the magnetic seeds of the sunflower follow the course of the Sun.[39] So by setting the plant afloat on the water, Kircher attempted to make a magnetic sundial.

37 Pettet, pp. 71-73.

38 Robert Fludd, *Mosaicall Philosophy* (London, 1659), p. 219.

39 Athanasius Kircher, *Magnes, sive De Arte Magnetica* (London, 1641), title page.

And Robert Fludd explains magnetism by using the concept of *emanatio*, which is a term derived from Neoplatonism, when he asks a rhetorical question:

> Is it not also a wonderfull Sympatheticall Emanation, that the Pigeon called the Carrier, doth make unto the place or dove-coat wherein he was bred and fostered? [40]

Similarly, in the poem 'Cock-Crowing', Vaughan says it is as if the magnetic bird knew the way to 'the house of light'. Many scholars have pointed out that the imagery of light in this poem is based on Hermetic philosophy.[41] In addition, however, considering, as I have pointed out in discussing 'Midnight', that in Vaughan's poems true faith manifests itself as magnetism and attracts light, we may argue that Vaughan's expressions relating to light may have political nuances.

For Vaughan as a Royalist, the contemporary circumstances of the 1640s and the 1650s are sometimes portrayed as a midnight. The light that existed in such a dark space, therefore, often represented false light rather than the true

40 *Ibid*., p. 228. 'Emanation' is defined, according to the *OED*, as 'The process of flowing forth, issuing, or proceeding from anything as a source . . . Often applied to the origination of created beings from God' (*OED* 1.)

41 See also Pettet, pp. 71-73, Elizabeth Holmes, *Henry Vaughan and the Hermetic Philosophy* (Oxford: Blackwell, 1932), p. 37.

light. For example, Peter Thomas points out that Quakers won converts in Wales by preaching the gospel of 'the indwelling light', and Philip West shows that '[t]he preaching of [Vavasor] Powell and his fellow "Welsh Saints" brought new light even to the remoter parts of Breconshire'. Indeed, '*new light*' was widely used 'as a handy tag for those whose views [were] thought unorthodox'.[42] That is why Vaughan himself says in 'The Night', that it is by the 'ill-guiding light' (l. 47) that the poet in this world 'Erre[s] more then [he] can do by night' (l. 48). It is an ignis fatuus, which is, in this religio- political context, the 'zeal' of puritan enthusiasm. In 'this sad night', the light in a Nativity poem written in 1656 is, paradoxically enough, not trustworthy:

> [. . .] what light is that doth stream,
> And drop here in a gilded beam?
> (Henry Vaughan, 'The Nativity, Written in the year 1656', ll. 31-32)

Vaughan moves in the world in which 'Satan himself is transformed into an angel of light' (2 Corinthians, 11-14). In this politically and religiously confused situation, the poet attacks Welsh Puritans who were known as the 'New Lights': 'Can these new lights be like to those, / These lights of Serpents like the Dove?' (White Sunday, ll. 9-10).[43] Thus, the poet comes to ask God to give human beings true light at the end of 'The Nativity, Written in the year 1656':

> Lord! grant some *Light* to us, that we
> May with them find the way to thee.
> Behold what mists eclipse the day:
> How dark it is ! shed down one *Ray*
> To guide us out of this sad night,
> And say once more, *Let there be Light.*
> (Henry Vaughan, 'The Nativity, Written in the year 1656', ll. 35-40)

Vaughan's plea for a truly new renovating light, '*Let there be Light*', can be taken as expressing his desire for the second advent of Christ. Vaughan's desire to expel the false light strengthens the anti-Puritan overtones of his poem. In addition, he associates magnetism with birds. This magnetic force is not only a metaphor, but also involves the power to resist the dominant political power of Puritans.

42 Peter Thomas, p. 27, West, pp. 155, 156. To borrow West's words, new light signifies 'the widespread Puritan belief that the Holy Spirit was making a fresh revelation of God to man, perhaps as a prologue to Christ's Second Coming' (p. 154).

43 See also West, pp. 149-150, 170-171.

Conclusion

What was magnetism for Vaughan? As a physician, who translated Henry Nollius's *Hermetical Physick* into English, Vaughan understood that magnets were a kind of medicine:

> Nature knowes better what is most convenient for her, then any Physician: for she makes use of her own proper fire, and Magnet, which attracts both from Physick and food, that which is congeneous, and most like to her selfe[.][44]

Furthermore, when we explore the full meaning of magnetism in Vaughan's poems, we cannot help considering the political situation in which he wrote. As we noted earlier, in the poem 'The Tempest', while other creatures ascend and descend between heaven and earth, man has lost his magnetic force and sleeps at the foot of 'Jacob's Ladder', which means that he has lost the way to his home. For Royalists, including Vaughan, their macrocosm was 'crumbled' and 'all dispers'd' (Henry Vaughan, 'Distraction', ll. 1, 2), especially after the execution of Charles I. They lost their ruler, and that confused world might be likened to the situation in which they had lost their own sense of direction. While the age was becoming exponentially involved in the maelstrom of war, Samuel Ward dedicated his book, *The Wonders of the Load-stone*, which was published in 1640, to Charles I. In the preface, he recommends to the king 'a Magnetick manner of Governing':

> Behold how the *Loadstone* subdues to it selfe all kind of Iron, which otherwise is scarce wrought upon, by files, hammers, and fiers, it is done, not by force of Armes, but by helpe of love. So the Iron is held in a dutifull subjection, being united together by the mutuall bonds of friendship; in like sort let the people see and consider with me how the Iron dust, that confused multitude, growes together into one body, under the *Loadstone*, as it were their King[.][45]

Trying to prevent armed conflict, Ward found some political meanings in the magnetic power, the directionality of which metaphorically teaches men their due course of action and brings about unity.

44 Heinrich Nollius, *Hermetic Physick: Englished by Henry Uaughan, Gent.* (London, 1655), p. 100.

45 Samuel Ward, *The Wonders of the Load-stone* (London,1640), sig. B4-B4v.

In the poem entitled 'The Queer', Vaughan asks what brings us joy, and answers in the final stanza:

> Sure, *holiness* the *Magnet* is[.]
>
> (Henry Vaughan, 'The Queer', l. 13)

The poet thinks that if he has true 'holiness', he can enjoy 'the high transcendent bliss', ('The Queer', l. 15). According to Vaughan, even stones have holiness. When the 'stones are deep in admiration' ('The Stone', l. 16), they can have 'commerce' with God:

> But I (Alas!)
> Was shown one day in a strange glass
> That busie commerce kept between
> God and his Creatures, though unseen.
>
> They hear, see, speak,
> And into loud discoveries break,
> As loud as blood. Not that God needs
> Intelligence, whose spirit feeds
> All things with life[.]
>
> (Henry Vaughan, 'The Stone', ll. 18-26)

Holiness on earth is brought about by true faith. As Vaughan describes it in such poems as 'Midnight' and 'The Constellation', he uses the image of true faith as a magnetic light as a means of criticizing the Puritans' 'new light' and their fanatical 'zeal'. The poet insists that true faith should have the power to attract and be attracted to heaven. This article has sought to show how one line of imagery in his work embodies the thought that the spiritual commerce between God and man's soul is tantamount to the magnetic force which works in two directions between heaven and earth. In Vaughan's description of men ascending to heaven by the power of magnets, we may find the poet's desire to regain a connection and re-establish the harmony between 'Man' and God. He may have sought for the mysterious power represented by and embodied in magnetism all the more because the world of his time was becoming politically dark and disorientated.

CHRISTOPHER NORRIS

Missing Hues

Wherever in the image of red and green stripes the observers looked, the colour they saw was 'simultaneously red and green', Crane and Piantanida wrote in their paper. Furthermore, 'some observers indicated that although they were aware that what they were viewing was a colour (that is, the field was not achromatic), they were unable to name or describe the colour. One of these observers was an artist with a large colour vocabulary'.

Natalie Wolchover

All shades conspire to hint at missing hues.
What though they're out of mind and out of sight?
Just spin the disc: it's paint-box shades you lose.

That's how the sense of shades unknown accrues
Each time the quick-spin colour-wheel turns white.
All shades conspire to hint at missing hues.

Let parrot-charts find room for cockatoos,
Pale plumage waving subtly in the light:
Just spin the disc: it's paint-box shades you lose.

Here, too, the colour-watcher may seek clues
To moods beyond the simply dark or bright.
All shades conspire to hint at missing hues.

Then there'll be spectral variants of the blues
With chords that set a darkling mood aright.
Just spin the disc: it's paint-box shades you lose.

Some say those shades are ones that artists use
Though nowhere marked on colour-charts packed tight.
All shades conspire to hint at missing hues.

Perhaps it's here that Newton pays his dues
To Goethe's *Farbenlehre* fancy-flight.
Just spin the disc: it's paint-box shades you lose.

So let your theory-choice depend on whose
Account allows that hues are infinite:
All shades conspire to hint at missing hues.

Yet spectrum-hoppers cannot pick and choose
Where best to land from some great theory-height.
Just spin the disc: it's paint-box shades you lose.

As bands dissolve so we should quit fixed views.
Let nuance reign, let differences be slight!
All shades conspire to hint at missing hues.

Why fear lest colour-boundaries blend and fuse?
Why let fixed views impose their nuance-blight?
Just spin the disc: it's paint-box shades you lose.

From what's most fugitive let's take our cues,
What's squint, oblique, opaque, half-glimpsed, not-quite:
All shades conspire to hint at missing hues.

For then maybe we'll figure what ensues
When nuance dawns as clearly as it might.
Just spin the disc: it's paint-box shades you lose;
All shades conspire to hint at missing hues.

ROSELLE ANGWIN

Before the World Turned Again

You won't remember but I do
that lone goose heading off over mill and leat;

the way that I knew we were finished
before we'd really begun. I was young –

early summer, full sun. I stood in the mown meadow
and watched the bird until my vision blurred.

That was the day of the hay-gyre that dervished
the new-cut grass in a twin helix up over the hills.

I watched how the drying hay borrowed wings,
eclipsed the speck of goose, blotted for a moment the sun.

Rooks

in the way I once might have
awaited a love   each morning
now I wait for your clamour
by the window   outside still
unresolved as if things as yet
unsure of the forms they want to take

you a mere black smudge of sound
a wave breaking raucous over
the unseen skyline like so much
dark acoustic dust now swelling
into emergent form

Messengers

you saved my sanity
that wild dark stormy dawn
after the night spent hunkered
beneath some rocky tor
as you had the wild dark stormy
dusk before

the harsh judder of your voices
welcome   reminding me
that the new is always waiting
to be born   and that the dark
too merits your jubilant applause

JONATHAN WOODING

Podcast

In memoriam Jacques Pohier (1926-2007)

Sunyolk in eggwhite welkin hides, leaving
only rose-of-Sharon still
to burn for autumn's shortening day;
furled flower-pods wait yet to unfold,
mocking our sun to run again

over sunflower seedheads buckling
and popping, dew-bowing grasses
bearing mercury-droplet rain,
unharvested Jerusalem artichokes,
and *every trifle my eyes detain.*

Rags of cloud occlude our turning wood –
(mutability is history without shame) – and
God is all over the place, it would appear,
as three scrotal red peppers gurn
from the glasshouse, over a dish of seeds,

a bowl of home-grown, doubtful toms,
and a grapevine on its knees –
detotalitarization of God, (O, Lord!):
Jacques' crown is broken, tumbling
with these leaves, beyond the pale.

LINDA SAUNDERS

Quahog

Ming the deep-sea clam was calculated to have been over 400 years old by scientists who counted the layers in his/her shell

Don't talk.
Think all the more.
Think therefore I clam.
Aye, long sum.
Times far done –
But who say world not turn down here?
It roll, it pull – moon tow,
deep stars too (O
Crab Nebula).
See?
No use for it.
But stuff drifts down.
Flake and flotsam, storm stew, wreck and bone.
Armada, Drake's drum.
Before my term?
Rumbles reach, water remember long.
Your god wars, bombs –
all so much thrum.
I keep my house in trim,
suit me snug.
And strong, has to be.
All own work pushed out from in,
and in be sleek and com-
fy, sure thing.
Each year I layer and lacquer.
All day open, wait what come,
sift, taste, rinse, shut up, padme hum.
There is a time for everything under the swim.

PATRICIA MCCARTHY

Discovery

(Iseult has been told by Tristan
about *Iseult-of-the white-hands)*

Doomsday when you told me.

Face down I lay, curving into the earth
instead of into you, trying not to separate
stone from shard and soil from root.
Drained of all colour at my dearth

the wild flowers kept up their heads,
words uniting into one damned flock,
even the good on fire as you turned
into penitents' racks our featherbeds.

No right had I to resent her being
myself by proxy: wasp-waisted,
no craters in her smile. Sudden masochisms
framed her in your arms, agreeing

to hold me down – while you led her
a smooth dance over our old roughings.
A soft successor she to offer griddle-scones
when you died over and over

to me in her ministry, mosquitoes exploding
the bluest samples of our blood
against her sides. Beating still in you,
my heart, for her setup, is imploding.

Review of *A Thickness of Particulars: The Poetry of Anthony Hecht* by Jonathan F.S. Post (Oxford University Press)

ANDREW NEILSON

Anthony Hecht (1923-2004) was a key figure among that generation of poets in the United States who were shaped by the experience – one might say 'pressure' – of following such pioneering luminaries of American verse as Robert Frost, Wallace Stevens, T.S. Eliot and Ezra Pound. In Hecht's case, it was Eliot who proved the most influential on his poetry – alongside the younger English example of W.H. Auden. Yet as his taste for Eliot and Auden might suggest, in truth Hecht's influences stretched back centuries into the canon of English literature. Shakespeare and Jonson, Donne and Herbert, were as important to this supremely accomplished formalist as any of his immediate predecessors, or older contemporaries such as Elizabeth Bishop and Robert Lowell.

Hecht's influences are cannily drawn out in this paperback edition of the first book-length study of his poetry, authored by Jonathan F.S. Post, Distinguished Professor of English at UCLA, editor of Hecht's Selected Letters, and a former student of the poet when he taught at the University of Rochester.

As Colm Tóibín has written in the London Review of Books, Anthony Hecht cannot be properly understood without recognising his status as a war poet. Hecht served in the Second World War and endured a number of traumatic episodes, including his involvement in the liberation of a concentration camp. Jonathan Post describes the true war poet as someone who can 'never be free of the subject, regardless of contemporary events' and indeed Hecht's verse is haunted throughout by his wartime experiences. Post addresses this head-on by commencing his study with a look at Hecht's harrowing sestina of the Holocaust, 'The Book of Yolek', before adopting a simpler chronological approach over the next two chapters, as each takes in one of Hecht's first two collections of poetry – including his breakthrough moment, the Pulitzer Prize-winning *The Hard Hours* (1967).

After this, however, Post rightly deploys a more thematic perspective as regards to Hecht's seminal output of the 1970s, when in the space of a few years this otherwise painstakingly slow writer published two of the finest volumes in post-war American poetry: *Millions of Strange Shadows* (1977) and *The Venetian Vespers* (1979). In doing so, Post is able to get under the skin of Hecht's various influences in much more detail, with entire chapters dedicated to Hecht's poetic camaraderie with his contemporary James Merrill, his absolute assimilation of Shakespearian concerns and language in a chapter delightfully titled 'Schechtspeare', and Hecht's longstanding interest in ekphrasis and his impressive mastery of rendering visual description in verse – a skill he acquired after much study of the work of Elizabeth Bishop.

A Thickness of Particulars is full of arresting insight and Jonathan Post marries a deep understanding of literary tradition to a sensitive examination of how Hecht sought to square up his own individual talent to that which had gone before. There is a telling moment when Post cites an essay from 1959 by one of Hecht's contemporaries, Donald Hall (who passed away in June 2018), which bemoans the way in which too many American poets write on 'domestic' themes, without the sense of history possessed by the likes of Eliot and Pound. The essay, published in American Scholar 28, reads rather shrilly today (as perhaps it did at the time) but the central contention remains as relevant as ever. Where does the poetry which will really last come from? Might it be situated in figures such as Anthony Hecht, who marshalled years of poetic study to grapple with all the majesty and horror of human history, or those who follow their 'frantic peer-group of the "six best poets now writing" and their poems and prefaces addressed to each other' (as Hall writes of the Beats)? In Jonathan Post's excellent critical study, we begin to discern the lineaments of an answer.

CONTRIBUTORS

ROSELLE ANGWIN is a poet, author and longstanding tutor in holistic writing courses. She has recently completed a new book, *A Spell in the Forest*, and is currently leading a yearlong 'Tongues in Trees' course.
www.roselle-angwin.co.uk www.thewildways.co.uk.

THOR BACON earned a BA in English from Antioch College in Ohio, USA. Recent poems appear in *The Aurorean*, *Qua Literary Journal*, and in the anthology, *If Bees Are Few*. He lives in Michigan, USA where he works as a goldsmith.

JOHN BARNIE is a poet, essayist, and former editor of *Planet, The Welsh Internationalist*. Two collections of poems, *Departure Lounge* (Cinnamon) and *Sherpas* (Rack Press) were published in 2018. *Sunglasses* (poems) will be published by Cinnamon in 2020. He plays guitar and blues.

ALISON BRACKENBURY has published ten collections of poetry. Her work has won an Eric Gregory and a Cholmondeley Award. Her Selected Poems, 'Gallop', was published in 2019 by Carcanet.

B. J. BUCKLEY is a Montana poet and writer who has been a teaching artist in Arts-in-Schools/Communities Programs in the western United States for more than 40 years. Her most recent book of poems is *Corvidae*: Poems of Ravens, Crows, and Magpies, Lummox press 2014.

MIRIAM CRAIG is a children's writer based in London. As well as *Scintilla* her poetry has appeared in *Obsessed With Pipework* and *Crossways*. She was part of the writing team who created *My Golden Ticket*, a children's book published by start-up Wonderbly in conjunction with the Roald Dahl Estate.

PRUE CHAMBERLAYNE, who grew up by the Severn, lives in London and the Aveyron in France. Her poems have been published in Acumen, Envoi, Orbis, Poetry Salzburg Review, Poetry Wales, Stand. Her first collection *Locks Rust* appeared in 2019.

OLIVER COMINS lives and works in West London. His first full-length collection, *Oak Fish Island*, was published in 2018 by Templar Poetry.

PAUL CONNOLLY's poems have appeared in *Agenda*, *The Warwick Review*, *Poetry Salzburg Review*, *The Reader*, *Envoi*, *Sarasvati*, *The Dawntreader*, *Dream Catcher*,

Orbis, *Canada Quarterly*, *The Journal*, *The Cannon's Mouth*, *Ink*, *Sweat & Tears*, *Foxtrot Uniform*, *Guttural*, *The Seventh Quarry*, and *Nine Muses*.

PAMELA COREN studied at the Universities of East Anglia and Kings' College London, and taught at the University of Leicester. Her critical work is on Renaissance poets, Gurney, Hopkins and Bunting, and she has one poetry collection, *The Blackbird Inspector* (2005). She is currently translating Li Qingzhao.

NEIL CURRY is a poet, translator and literary critic with a particular interest in the 18th century, having published books on Alexander Pope, Christopher Smart and William Cowper. He has published nine collections of poetry, most recently, *On Keeping Company with Mrs Woolf.*

WILLIAM VIRGIL DAVIS's most recent book is Dismantlements of Silence: Poems Selected and New. Earlier books are: The Bones Poems; Landscape and Journey (New Criterion Poetry Prize and Helen C. Smith Memorial Award for Poetry); Winter Light; The Dark Hours (Calliope Press Chapbook Prize); One Way to Reconstruct the Scene (Yale Series of Younger Poets Prize).

ROSE FLINT, writer and art therapist, worked as a creative writing tutor and is now part of the multi-arts team, Elevate, working in elderly care. She has six collections, most recently *Mapping the Borders,* winner of the Littoral Press prize. She won the Cardiff Poetry Prize and the Petra Kenney International Prize.

TOM GOUTHWAITE. Biography unavailable.

CHRIS HALL's work has appeared in *Scintilla*, *Tears in the Fence, The Lonely Crowd,* and *Quirk*. His poem *why i do not play cricket* was also recently included in Richard Parker's anthology on cricket, *Leg Avant* published by Crater (2016). The collection *No Fish* is due to be published this year.

MARC HARSHMAN's collection, *WOMAN IN RED ANORAK*, won the Blue Lynx Poetry Prize from Lynx House/University of Washington [2018]. *BELIEVE WHAT YOU CAN,* West Virginia University Press, won the Weatherford Award from the Appalachian Studies Association. He is the poet laureate of West Virginia.

GRAHAM HARTILL is a former poetry editor for *Scintilla* with Anne Cluysenaar and Hilary Llewellyn-Williams. He is writer in residence in HMP Parc, Bridgend. His latest poetry collection is a collaborative translation (with Professor Wu Fusheng, University of Utah): *The Seven Masters of the Jian'an Era.*

MICHAEL HENRY has published four collections with Enitharmon Press and one, his latest, *Bureau of the Lost and Found*, with Five Seasons Press. He has been widely published in magazines and in 2011 he won the Hippocrates Open Prize for a medical poem.

RIC HOOL has 9 collections of published poetry and has his work featured in poetry magazines & journals in Europe, USA & UK. His 10th collection, *Personal Archaeology*, will be published April 2020. He is from Northumberland but lives in Wales.

EVE JACKSON is a poet living in Bembridge, Isle of Wight. She is a winner of the Frogmore Poetry prize and a runner-up in the Manchester Cathedral competition. She is also a regular contributor to the *Poems in the Waiting Room*.

ROSIE JACKSON lives in rural Somerset. *What the Ground Holds* (Poetry Salzburg, 2014) was followed by *The Light Box* (Cultured Llama, 2016) and *The Glass Mother: A Memoir* (Unthank, 2016). Poetry awards include 1st prize at Wells 2018, and 2nd prize at Torbay 2018. www.rosiejackson.org.uk

MIKE JENKINS is a Retired teacher who blogs regularly on his website www.mike jenkins.net. He is former editor of *Poetry Wales* & co-editor *Red Poets* for 25 years. His latest book of poetry is From *Aberfan t Grenfell* (Culture Matters) with Swansea artist Alan Perry.

VICKI KAY, a four-time winner of the John Danby Prize for English Literature, is a PhD student at Bangor University, Wales. She researches the appropriation of mercantile practice and language in late medieval and early modern women's writing, including letters, life-writing, accounts, and wills. Vicki is particularly interested in late medieval and early modern women's involvement with business and money: how much did they spend and on what? What did they invest in? What did they sell? What did they bequeath, and to whom and why?

FRANCES-ANNE KING is an award winning poet and editor. Her poems have been published in national and International Journals. In 2018 she won Ist prize in the St Hilda's College Oxford, SciPo poetry competition. She lives in Bath where she facilitates poetry workshops for the Holburne Museum.

S. A. LEAVESLEY is a prize-winning poet, fiction writer, journalist and photographer. Her latest books include *Always Another Twist* (Mantle Lane, novella), as well as *How to Grow Matches* (Against The Grain, poetry) and *plenty-fish* (Nine Arches, poetry). Website: http://sarah-james.co.uk

EMMA LEE's recent collection is "Ghosts in the Desert" (IDP). "The Significance of a Dress" is forthcoming from Arachne (UK). She co-edited "Over Land, Over Sea," (Five Leaves), and reviews for *The Blue Nib*, *High Window Journal*, *The Journal*, *London Grip*, *Sabotage Reviews*. http://emmalee1.wordpress.com.

PETER LIMBRICK is an educationalist interested in babies who have neurological impairment. He lives near Hay-on-Wye and aspires to a Buddhist view of life and death.

GREVEL LINDOP has published seven collections of poems with Carcanet, including *Selected Poems* (2001) and *Luna Park* (2015). His award-winning biography *Charles Williams: The Third Inkling* came out from OUP in 2015. He is writing a book about the spiritual life and poetry of W.B. Yeats. www.grevel.co.uk

SARAH LINDON's poems have appeared in magazines including *Agenda*, *Magma*, *Oxford Poetry*, *Poetry Wales*, *Stand*, *The Interpreter's House* and *The Reader*. She has an MPhil in Writing from the University of Glamorgan, and lives and works in London.

MAI MATSUMOTO is Assistant Professor of Literature in English at Hiroshima University in Japan. She is the author of *Henry Vaughan and the Philosopher's Stone* (Kinseido, 2016 [Japanese]). She is currently working on the relationship between Early Modern Science and English Literature.

PATRICIA MCCARTHY, editor of *Agenda* (www.agendpapoetry.co.uk) won the National Poetry Competition 2013. Previous collections include *Rodin's Shadow*, *Horses Between Our Legs*, and *Letters to Akhmatova. Trodden Before* (High Window Press), and *Rockabye* (Worple Press) have very recently been published.

SEAN H. MCDOWELL is Associate Professor of English at Seattle University, where he currently serves as Director of the University Honors Program. He is the author of numerous essays on Shakespeare, Donne, Herbert, Vaughan, and their contemporaries and as well as on modern Irish and American poets. He is the Executive Director of the John Donne Society and the editor of the *John Donne Journal*. His poems have appeared in *Poetry Ireland Review*, *The Lyric*, *The High Window*, *Cirque: A Literary Journal for the North Pacific Rim*, *Scintilla*, *The Best of Vine Leaves Literary Journal 2014*, and *Clover, a literary rag*, among other venues.

BRUCE MCRAE has published over 1,400 poems internationally in magazines such as *Poetry*, *Rattle and the North American Review*. His books are *The So-Called Sonnets* (Silenced Press), *An Unbecoming Fit Of Frenzy* (Cawing Crow Press) and *Like As If* (Pski's Porch), *Hearsay* (The Poet's Haven).

HELEN MOORE is an award-winning socially engaged ecopoet and artist. She has two poetry collections, *Hedge Fund, And Other Living Margins* (Shearsman Books, 2012) and *ECOZOA* (Permanent Publications, 2015). Her third collection, *The Mother Country,* is due in 2019. www.helenmoorepoet.com

HUBERT MOORE Hubert Moore's latest collection is 'The tree line' (Shoestring, 2017). 'The feeding-station', his tenth, is due this summer, also from Shoestring.

OLIVER MORT is from Belfast. His work has appeared in *The Rialto, Wasafiri, Poetry Ireland Review, Poetry Salzburg, Envoi, The Yellow Nib*, and elsewhere.

PAUL MURPHY was born in Belfast in 1965. He studied at Warwick and Queen's, Belfast. He has published four pamphlets, one book of poetry (*In the Luxembourg Gardens*, University of Salzburg Press), a book of criticism *T. S. Eliot's Post-Modernist Complaint*, Postpressed, Australia.

CAROLINE NATZLER collections are *Design Fault* (Flambard) and *Smart Dust* (Grenadine). She has published three pamphlet collections, *Fold* (Hearing Eye), *Only* and *Still* (both Grenadine). She teaches creative writing at the City Lit in London and also runs private workshops.

JONATHAN NAUMAN's Vaughan Colloquium presentation on "Varying Arrangements" in Silex Scintillans (1655) has recently been reprinted by the Huntington Library Quarterly. An article on "Composition as Exploration" has just emerged in Sub-Creating Arda: World-Building in J. R. R. Tolkien's Work, its Precursors, and its Legacies (Zurich and Jena, 2019).

ANDREW NEILSON has contributed poems and essays to *The Dark Horse*, *New Writing Scotland*, *The Poetry Review* and the Scottish Poetry Library's *Best Scottish Poems 2017*. Contributions are forthcoming in *Stand* and *The Hopkins Review*. Born in Edinburgh, he lives and works in London.

CHRISTOPHER NORRIS, Emeritus Professor of Philosophy at Cardiff University, Wales, taught English Literature and Philosophy. He has written books about philosophy, literary theory, music, and the history of ideas. His recent poetry includes *For the Tempus-Fugitives*, *The Matter of Rhyme*, and *The Trouble with Monsters*.

CHRIS PREDDLE's third collection, *The May Figures*, is forthcoming (Eyewear). His second collection was *Cattle Console Him* (Waywiser, 2010). His work has appeared in Scintilla, and in *Irish Pages*, *PN Review*, *Poetry London*, *The Poetry Review*, *The Shop*, *Stand*, *The Yellow Nib* and other magazines.

JONATHAN F. S. POST, Distinguished Research Professor of English, University of California, Los Angeles, is the author of *Henry Vaughan: The Unfolding Vision* (Princeton University Press, 1982). His most recent books include *The Oxford Handbook of Shakespeare's Poetry* (Oxford, 2013, rpt. 2016), *The Selected Letters of Anthony Hecht* (Johns Hopkins, 2013), *A Thickness of Particulars: The Poetry of Anthony Hecht* (Oxford, 2015; rpt. 2018), and *Shakespeare's Sonnets and Poems: A Very Short Introduction* (Oxford, 2017). He has been a Fellow of the Folger Shakespeare Library, the National Endowment of the Humanities, The John Simon Guggenheim Memorial Foundation, and the Bogliasco Foundation in Genoa, Italy.

LAWRENCE SAIL is a Fellow of the Royal Society of Literature. His *Waking Dreams: New & selected Poems* (Bloodaxe Books, 2010) was a Poetry Book Society Special Commendation. *The Quick* (also from Bloodaxe) came out in 2015. A new collection, *Guises*, is due from Bloodaxe early in 2020.

LESLEY SAUNDERS has published several books of poems and works with visual artists, dancers and musicians. A poetry collaboration with Philip Gross, *A Part of the Main*, designed by artist Valerie Coffin Price and published by Mulfran Press, came out in 2018.

LINDA SAUNDERS has been widely published in magazines and anthologies, including *New Women Poets* from Bloodaxe Books. Her first full-length collection was short-listed for the Jerwood Aldeburgh Prize, and her most recent book, *A Touch on the Remote*, is published by Worple Press.

JOSEPHINE SCOTT has two poetry collections; *Sparkle and Dance*, and *Rituals*, both published by Red Squirrel Press. Her third, *When Rain is Memory* will be published in May 2020. She is a contributor to *This Cullercoats* anthology, which is to be launched at the *Iron in the Soul Festival* in June 2019.

ELIZABETH SIBERRY is a historian based in Breconshire. She coedited Henry Vaughan and the Usk Valley (Logaston, 2016) and is a regular contributor to Brycheiniog, writing about a series of individuals who lived in the Usk Valley in the eighteenth and nineteenth centuries. She is also a Trustee of the National Library of Wales; a member of the Council of the University of Wales Trinity Saint David and the Executive Council of the Brecknock Society and Museum Friends.

THOMAS R. SMITH's most recent poetry collections are *The Glory* (Red Dragonfly Press) and *Windy Day at Kabekona* (White Pine Press). He has edited *Airmail: The Letters of Robert Bly and Tomas Tranströmer* (Bloodaxe). He lives in western Wisconsin and posts poems and essays at www.thomasrsmithpoet.com.

SEÁN STREET is Emeritus Professor at Bournemouth University. Recent poetry is *Camera Obscura* (Rockingham), and prose is *Sound at the Edge of Perception: the Aural Minutiae of Sand and Other Worldly Murmurings* (Palgrave, 2019). He has written works on Gerard Manley Hopkins and The Dymock Poets.

KAY SYRAD is Poetry Editor for *Envoi*. Recent publications include an anthology, *Poemish and Other Languages* (edited with Clare Whistler, Elephant, 2019), a novel, *Send* (Cinnamon, 2015), a collaboration with land artist Chris Drury, *Exchange* (Little Toller, 2015) and *Inland* (Cinnamon, 2018).

CHARLES WILKINSON's poems have been in *Poetry Wales*, *Tears in the Fence*, *Scintilla* and other journals. A pamphlet, *Ag & Au*, came out from Flarestack Poets in 2013; two collections of weird fiction and strange tales, from Egaeus Press. A poetry collection, *The Glazier's Choice*, will appear from Eyewear in 2020.

MARGARET WILMOT, born in California, she has worked in the Mediterranean and New York before moving to Sussex, UK, in 1978. Her poems have been published in

Acumen, *Artemis*, *Magma*, *Oxford Poetry*, *Rialto*, *Scintilla*, *Smiths-Knoll*, *Staple*, and *Temenos*. A book is due out summer 2019, by *The High Window*.

JONATHAN WOODING is a WEA tutor. Cantos from his *Psalm 119* can be found online at *Cassandra Voices*, and in *Scintilla 21*.

HOWARD WRIGHT lectures at the Ulster University, Belfast. He is twice winner of The Frogmore Prize and was awarded second prize in last year's Ver Poets Open and Commended in the McLellan Prize. Poems have since appeared in *Obsessed with Pipework*, *Cyphers* and *Abridged* (Derry).

THE ARTIST

COLIN SEE-PAYTON is a Fellow of the Royal Cambrian Academy, Honorary Fellow of the Royal Society of Painter-Printmakers and a member of the Society of Wood Engravers. He is widely regarded as the leading exponent of wood engraving in the United Kingdom and his work is represented in many private and public collections around the world including the V & A, Ashmolean Museum, Berlin Graphothek, Fremantle Museum & Art Gallery, Australia, Gaudi Salon, Barcelona, Guangdong Museum of Art, China, National Library of Wales, National Museum of Wales and the Yosemite Wildlife Museum, California. He has travelled with the Artists for Nature Foundation to the Pyrenees and to Alaska to record and highlight through his art the threat to wildlife caused by man's exploitation of the natural resources of these areas. The Ashmolean Museum has recently added more of Colin's wood engravings to this important public collection and now holds over one hundred pieces. To find out more visit www.see-paynton.co.uk.

Printed in Great Britain
by Amazon